M000079579

SHUT HELL UP

SHUT HELL UP

REAL TALK KIM

CHARISMA HOUSE

Most Charisma House Book Group products are available at special quantity discounts for bulk purchase for sales promotions, premiums, fund-raising, and educational needs. For details, call us at (407) 333-0600 or visit our website at www.charismahouse.com.

SHUT HELL UP by Real Talk Kim
Published by Charisma House
Charisma Media/Charisma House Book Group
600 Rinehart Road, Lake Mary, Florida 32746

Unless otherwise noted, all Scripture quotations are from the New King James Version of the Bible. Copyright © 1979, 1980, 1982 by Thomas Nelson, Inc. Used by permission. All rights reserved.

Scripture quotations marked AMP are from the Amplified Bible. Copyright © 2015 by The Lockman Foundation. Used by permission. www.Lockman.org

Scripture quotations marked ESV are from the Holy Bible, English Standard Version. Copyright © 2001 by Crossway Bibles, a division of Good News Publishers. Used by permission.

Scripture quotations marked KJV are from the King James Version of the Bible.

Scripture quotations marked MSG are from *The Message: The Bible in Contemporary English,* copyright © 1993, 1994, 1995, 1996, 2000, 2001, 2002. Used by permission of NavPress Publishing Group.

Scripture quotations marked NIV are taken from the Holy Bible, New International Version®, NIV®. Copyright © 1973, 1978, 1984, 2011 by Biblica, Inc.® Used by permission of Zondervan. All rights reserved worldwide. www.zondervan.com. The "NIV" and "New International Version" are trademarks registered in the United States Patent and Trademark Office by Biblica, Inc.®

Scripture quotations marked NLT are from the Holy Bible, New Living Translation, copyright © 1996, 2004, 2007. Used by permission of Tyndale House Publishers, Inc., Carol Stream, Illinois 60188. All rights reserved.

All emphasis is the author's own.

Testimonies used with permission.

Copyright © 2020 by Real Talk Kim (Kimberly Jones-Pothier)
All rights reserved

Visit the author's website at realtalkkim.com.

Library of Congress Cataloging-in-Publication Data:
An application to register this book for cataloging has been submitted to the Library of Congress.

International Standard Book Number: 978-1-62999-725-4
E-book ISBN: 978-1-62999-726-1

20 21 22 23 24 — 987654321
Printed in the United States of America

Contents

Acknowledgments

FIRST, I WOULD like to say thank you to my family who covers me in prayer daily and keeps me centered in real time as I travel weekly. During our family get-togethers, we just let our hair down and laugh with one another. You bring me back to reality as we meet and eat, yet you support me in every way, even packing and shipping products. We play hard and work hard! I wouldn't have chosen any other family to live life with but you. Mark, Morgan and Lyncoln, Dad and Mom, Rob and Melissa—you guys were chosen by God to be an integral part of my life today. Mom, we did it again—-finished another book to give God all the glory!

Second, I would like to thank the thousands of social media followers who keep me on my toes as I am seeking God daily for a fresh rhema word for you. I have become a much better person as a result of transparency. I realize honesty is the most important attribute I have, so I want to make sure that I give you tidbits that will assist you in living your best life yet. Thank you for accepting me as I am.

Last but not least, I am so thankful for my dedicated

staff who answers hundreds of calls weekly for invitations to preach. Besides working the schedule, you are always thinking ahead on how to make life easier as I travel thousands of miles each week. You are all amazing!

Of course, I give God all the glory. Without His anointing, I could not and would not be doing what I do. My greatest gift is His salvation for me, which set me up to live my best life now.

Introduction

EVERY ONE OF us deals with chatter in the psyche—voices that tear us down and stir up fear. Recognizing the effect of these voices in framing our lives is a game changer. I know, because until I was in my late thirties, I had a choir of inner chatterboxes telling me how insecure, intimidated, and useless I was. They succeeded in ruling my daily life for decades. But the moment I chose to shut them down, I tasted a freedom I never knew I could have.

Why had I allowed aimless conversations in my head to distract my purpose for so long when choosing to change took only a moment? I'd fought the battle in my mind from the first grade all the way to age thirty-six. I had no idea that the enemy kept me broken just by stealing my focus.

When I reached my rock bottom, however, I found the answer to my whys and realized why my future had always turned out like my past: it was because I kept bringing my past with me! That's when I learned to shut up the hell that tormented me day and night.

I am an authority on how the tormented mind leads

to failure because I lived it. However, I no longer have to embrace that life—and neither do you. When you control your thoughts, you control your life. The truth is, you become what you think of most of the time. So becoming free is all about changing the channel in your mind from confusion and doubt to the things God says about you. No, I don't think you can do it alone. But I know with everything in me that, through Christ, you can do all things. I am a living example of how He turns a broken mess into a message. Therefore, I fully believe that Jesus wants to turn your misery into a ministry too.

It will take some cooperation on your part. It's too easy to say we trust God and then try to handle the situation ourselves. God is always working for our good, but He gave us a say in things. If we keep trying to control everything, we limit what He'll do for us. Even when Jesus was with His disciples, in the flesh and working miracles, the people of Nazareth limited Him. They thought they knew who He was—the son of a carpenter instead of the Son of God. Their unbelief prevented Him from delivering good news and performing miracles in His hometown. So, Jesus just moved on. I think He did it because God respects the free will He gave to humanity. He is a gentleman who never forces us to believe Him.

Unbelief comes in many forms. During the years when my life was breaking apart, I tried to look like a strong Christian, so I seldom revealed my weaknesses. But at rock bottom I discovered that the strongest Christians are quick to admit their frailties and look to God. The more I did this, the more

He got involved in my life. Now when I'm up against it, I say, "Jesus in me can make this happen."

We need to realize that our unbelief limits God's power and prevents it from doing its work in us. Paul said in Philippians 4:13 that we can do all things through Christ who strengthens us. It's not Jesus Christ who limits us. We do it to ourselves. That's why it's so important to discover who God is in our lives. When we do, we find out who we are. Then we can quit struggling with the insecurities and self-promotion that define much of society.

Are you hearing me? You no longer have to measure up or qualify. You are free to be yourself. That doesn't mean being perfect. You have failures in your life, and so do I. That's why I can totally relate to what Steven Furtick said:

> I used to think that the answer to my failures was to fix them, that the solution to my weaknesses was to replace them with strengths. I assumed the secret to success was to appear as perfect, flawless, and superhuman as possible. I concluded that my character and my competency qualified or disqualified me.[1]

I have been there. Now finally, I have allowed Jesus Christ to be Lord of my life. Therefore, I can see myself as He sees me, and I love the me I see. His view of who I am gives me the freedom and self-confidence to speak to thousands of people about the love of God.

For the record, the confidence you desire will never come from your qualifications anyway. "You could never be perfect enough or failproof enough to be at peace with yourself on that basis alone. Peace and confidence come through one thing: acceptance. . . . That means confronting the parts of you that you may prefer to ignore. And it means knowing who you are (and who you are not) in and through Jesus."[2]

Acceptance starts with "God's unconditional acceptance of you" as His child. When you understand that He loves you in spite of your imperfections, then you will accept yourself and His "process of change" in you. You see, when God works in and through you, He's not trying to make you into somebody else; He wants to "bring out the best possible version of you."[3] God will not bless the person you "pretend to be." But He will bless the person you are—the one He created for this day.[4] So don't allow the enemy to put you down and make you believe that you are less than the best any longer.

Shut hell up.

As you journey with me through these pages, remember who I am—a woman who used to be like Cruella de Vil. I was coldhearted, full of venom and hurt. Honestly, what you see today is the result of countless hours spent with the Lord as He reconditions me to be *me*. I can't tell you how many times people on social media have asked, "Is this really the Kimberly Jones who went to high school with me?"

They remember the girl dancing on the bar. Now I am the woman who's walking it straight and leading thousands to God. It didn't happen overnight. I remember a vision the Lord gave me back when I realized I wanted total change. I told Him that I was finished—finished with the life I was living, finished with all the bitterness and pain I carried. That night, God literally transformed me—*totally*. In that vision He showed me coming out of my body and slipping into the body of a woman in a catlike lacquer bodysuit with thigh-high boots.

I've never been able to wear such an outfit except in this vision. I saw myself destroying everything in my path as I walked. The Lord told me He had used everything in my life that I detested to bring me to that day. He told me I would no longer be a destroyer but a healer—someone who could point people toward the change they wanted.

God showed me my past in order to take me into my future. As you journey with me through *Shut Hell Up,* make up your mind that your time for total transformation is now. It's your choice to make.

Part I: The Stuck Place

CHAPTER 1

Ruled by Emotions

DO YOUR EMOTIONS ever get in your way? Have you experienced a trauma or disappointment that knocked you out of your lane and into survival mode? I know I have—and I know I'm not alone. When I minister each week, I look into the eyes of emptiness, indecision, and even desire—the desire for things to change. I see them through my own pain, which was caused by other people's expectations and the belief system I based on my assumptions about life.

Realizing that most of us are ruled by our emotions helps me understand those who reach out to me. To stand and tell them what I believe God is saying about their situations brings me back to the life challenges He has allowed me to go through—challenges that have caused me to be a strong, bullheaded female in a male-dominated world. Have you noticed that there's plenty of potential for drama in life? I have. So, I tell myself, "Save the drama for your— Never mind, girl. Just save the drama!" As a female, I will not allow my emotions to control my outcomes. I have determined that life is not all about my feelings. To live and work among strong men and women means to suck it up while deciding that life is not always about me. This creates a whole different attitude as I arise daily and give the Lord permission to be Lord and Savior in every area of my life.

That's my self-talk most days. Listen, our emotions are the worst drivers where our decisions are concerned. Yet we let them drive us most of the time, even when they're toxic. That's how the majority of our mistakes happen. They are just bad decisions that add up and eventually determine our destination. Then our toxicity teams up with our failures to cause a sense of inadequacy—all while we are trying to figure out what's next.

Emotional Choices

Feelings of inadequacy are powerful drivers of behavior and can trigger decision-making that derails our best intentions. That's because the choices they trigger come from places of doubt and insecurity instead of confidence and purposeful determination.

Have I allowed emotional choices to be my greatest motivator? Absolutely! I did it through most of my life. Although those choices might have determined my destination, I switched tracks and started a journey of freedom. From where I sit now, I can look back and see where my feelings of inadequacy took control of my emotions. It was so early in my childhood that it became my norm and the foundation for years of decision-making.

As a preacher's kid in a family of preachers, I understood a certain order of life: God, church, and family. Immediately after my parents got married, they hit the road in full-time evangelism, moving from city to city and staying with pastors. Once my brother and I came along, our family called a travel trailer home. When I was two and my brother was about to start school, we settled in a small Mississippi town to start a new church. The life we had known till then totally changed.

The Joneses were always seen together. Even when our parents went out for the evening, my brother and I were their permanent "plus two." Our parents were always very selective of our influencers. Honestly, my brother and I never had a babysitter. Mom and Dad had to approve even the kids we played with. I did not always like feeling confined this way, but looking back, I realize what our parents were doing. They provided us a safe place to call home, and they protected us from anyone and anything that would cause us harm.

It was a noble cause. But as we all know, there is no way to keep anyone safe from everything all the time. That's just a fact of life. As attentive as my parents were, they could not protect me from feelings of inadequacy. As I look back, I am amazed at how early I became burdened with those feelings. When I was seven, I asked Jesus into my heart because I did not want to go to hell. Even though I took that step, I never pursued a personal and fruitful relationship with Christ. Nor did I acknowledge His love and wisdom. My parents continually told me what Psalm 139:14 said about my being "fearfully and wonderfully made." But, for some reason, it never sank in.

The Power of Labels

From the moment I walked into elementary school, my identity as a wonderfully made human being seemed lost forever. Every task seemed beyond me—from learning my vocabulary words to math to reading. Inadequacy plagued me as I saw my classmates advancing easily while I floundered. I felt completely isolated and even forgotten.

No wonder my mother faced a battle when she dropped me off at school each morning. She (literally) had to wrestle with me to get me out of the car. It was so bad that the principal would meet us and escort me into her office, where I would eventually calm down enough to go to class. Once the day's lessons got underway, I felt even more humiliated as my classmates watched me stumble through my phonics. The whole experience was terrifying, and I'm sure I opened many emotional doors in those dark moments. Unfortunately, those openings allowed the formation of strongholds that lasted longer than I care to admit.

My parents had no idea what to do when I barely passed first grade. Then we moved to Atlanta, where the journey started over again in a new school. After the first week of classes, my mother scheduled a conference with my teacher, who was already sensing that I would need special assistance.

That is when we first heard the term *learning disability*. It became my identity from that point until I entered high school. Each day, my teacher would call out my name for tutoring. Honestly, I thought for years that I was some kind of VIP who was being dismissed for special attention while the other kids were stuck in one classroom all day. Then one day my teacher accidentally mentioned that my special dismissal was for learning-disabled kids. I stayed in my seat thinking, "She's definitely not talking to me."

But she was, and now the whole world knew that I was a learning-disabled child who needed extra help. I can't begin to explain the heartbreak I felt or how crushed I was at the time. But those feelings instantly overtook my life. Everybody knew that something was wrong with me. I would never be like other kids, and I would never measure up.

My parents moved me to a popular Christian school around that time, thinking this could be the answer for me. They had no idea that it would lead to an even darker season of inadequacy so overwhelming that I could hardly breathe. When I looked around my classroom, I saw students drooling and even wetting themselves. I began questioning myself and looking in the mirror to see whether I was the girl I thought I was. Maybe I was drooling and didn't know it. Maybe I was so mentally challenged that I could not recognize the extent of my disability.

During recess, I would look out the window and see my brother and his friends playing like "normal" kids. I think that had the greatest impact on me. I can still rehearse the pain of feeling set apart, and I realize how situations in life can royally mess you up.

After being in despair for some time, I finally came clean with my parents about how crushed I was. I promised that if they would return me to public school, I would do everything I could to measure up and be the daughter they deserved. Thank God they truly loved me and wanted what was best for me. They did not burden me with expectations I could not handle. They continually supported me and spoke life into every situation. I can tell you right now that my mother was like an angel disguised as a woman.

At the time, I thought that I was failing my family and myself. I did not understand that my situation had nothing to do with my being good or bad. I simply faced challenges with learning. For one thing, I struggled to remember what I studied. My mom spent hours every night rehearsing spelling words and math problems with me. Yet I would fail my tests the next day. I was tormented with wondering why I couldn't be normal and couldn't get it together. It was especially hard because my brother breezed through school. He didn't even have to study to make great grades.

You will never conquer . . . what you refuse to confront.

"Why, God?" I would ask. "Why me?"

One of my favorite scriptures will always be Jeremiah 29:11: "For I know the thoughts that I think toward you, says the LORD, thoughts of peace and not of evil, to give you a future and a hope." To this day, it lets me know that God has a plan just for me. It reminds me that even when I could not see my future, He was taking care of me.

When I entered the eighth grade, my parents moved me back to public school. Immediately, the school placed me in a learning-disabled study group. Amazingly enough, I continued to dream of being normal. I learned from author John Hagee that "you will never conquer...what you refuse to confront."[1] So I became determined to do my best and kept reminding my mom that when I got to high school, I would be normal. All I needed was a chance to prove that I could be the daughter they deserved. My promise gave me a goal, but it did not silence the running dialogue in my head. One voice said I was fearfully and wonderfully made; the other still questioned whether I could overcome the label *learning disabled*.

In my book *Beautifully Broken,* I talk about the voices that attack children who are not yet equipped to resist them:

> During the traumatic times in our childhood, we were open to the still small voices of evil spirits. When we heard them, we thought they were our own thoughts, since we had no wisdom yet to consider otherwise. The demonic forces plants feelings of rejection, causing us to become shameful and self-rejection, self-hatred, and bitterness are then produced.
>
> Then the spirits set up a protective mechanism against these feelings, usually in the form of blame shifting.[2]

When you understand that you have an enemy that continually tears you down and encourages a false self-image, you have the ammunition you need to defeat him. But you might not get that revelation right away. Instead, you might do what many of us have done: we become "blind to our faults and the unveiling of our true feelings," in part because they seem "to only bring us more shame" and feelings of inadequacy.[3]

To avoid our shame, we stuff our feelings and act as though we have the world by the tail. But living a lie can't comfort us. It only paralyzes us. I like to say that the scariest place to be is believing our own lies. What we need is not to cover our pain but to go after our full healing. We might be on the verge of breaking a generational curse and not even know it. That could be why the attacks have been so hard. We need to stay focused and not crumble with every hit, because if trauma can be passed down through generations, so can healing.

I know that when I am being my craziest, loudest, brashest

self, people wonder who I am. Why do I have to be the loudest one on the platform, always jumping and running and praising? Believe me—I even talk to myself and tell the loud me to calm down and be quiet. "Deliver your message like other women who are so graceful," I tell myself.

But when I begin speaking, I find myself shouting and moving like crazy all over again. I think it's because I have come from such a difficult place. I just want to give everything within me to the Creator who changed my life and gave me this opportunity to change my world.

Lay It Down

Do you feel stuck in certain areas of your life? Maybe God is waiting for you to lay down something so He can finally move. Just as a physical move requires you to leave something behind, so does a spiritual move. What are you desperately clutching that you need to release? God is waiting for you to obey Him. He wants to move in your life. Don't let stubbornness or even inadequacy keep you from His blessings.

Psalm 37:23–24 says that "the steps of a good man are ordered by the LORD, and He delights in his way. Though he fall, he shall not be utterly cast down; for the LORD upholds him with His hand." When I found this beautiful scripture, it transformed me. But it was much later in my life. If I can open your understanding to the greatness of God's Spirit guiding and directing you despite your failures, you will be way ahead of the struggle I faced all those years. When you realize, like I finally did, that God is in the middle of every struggle, you will stop fighting what doesn't work.

God is opening a better way!

I remember sitting in a counseli
instructor brought forward a young
molested as a child. He explained th
seling, she would have to rehearse t
the ultimate point of counseling is to
accepted as truth. That's because our anger, depression, and languishing are rooted in lies about what we have heard and experienced.

The instructor wanted this woman to visualize the room where the molestation happened. As she began weeping, he asked her to look around that room and reveal what she saw. She explained that she saw Jesus in the midst of the worst time of her life. He was with her, responding to her crisis. That was a revelation because she had always believed she was alone in her pain. Now she was open to believing that Jesus *never* left her and never forsook her, even during her most terrible times. She also discovered that she was not the culprit in her molestation. She was just a child at the mercy of an unscrupulous relative.

If trauma can be passed down through generations, so can healing.

That wounded young woman had allowed a painful experience to direct much of her life. She had been unable to have a solid relationship with a man because she thought she did not deserve such a relationship. Now the light exposed the lies she had believed, and healing became possible.

Hearing her story helped me to look inside my own pain. Like her, I realized that I had not caused the crisis that directed my life for so long. Finally, I could say, "Not today, devil!" No will I allow the pain that I experienced throughout my dhood to determine the direction I travel as an adult.

Lies Are Just Lies

You see, unless God's light is shed on painful events from the past, we tend to believe the lies those events suggest. As long as the lies remain hidden, they distort our thinking, emotions, and beliefs about God's goodness. The answer is to expose them to the truth of God's Word and His mercy. Once you do that, you can experience a freedom that will change your life.

I can tell you that I waited too many years to understand all the pain I was carrying. Therefore, the pain continued to manipulate and control my every move, until—*finally*—at the age of thirty-six, I began the journey toward freedom. I definitely don't want you to wait as long as I did to release everyone and everything that may be stunting your growth!

It's time to dump the lies and walk in the confidence that truth brings—the confidence that we are beautifully and wonderfully made by God, and He is ordering our steps. I really believe that when we *get* this, our lives become a whole lot easier. If you have followed my ministry for any length of time, you know that, to me, the most important thing is being who God created me to be. I didn't always understand that. But once I did, I discovered my identity and I no longer struggled with the insecurities that had long burdened me. I quit straining to measure up or qualify, because I was free to be *me*.

There was a time when being me wasn't what I wanted. I kept trying to fix myself and hide my weaknesses. I spent way too much time becoming "perfect" and missed what my life was all about. Instead of being confident, I felt disqualified. Even so, I was a work in progress.[4] As I read Philippians chapter 4, Paul's words reached me. He was talking about having a kind of peace that could not even be understood.

> Don't worry about anything; instead, pray about everything. Tell God what you need, and thank him for all he has done. Then you will experience God's peace, which exceeds anything we can understand. His peace will guard your hearts and minds as you live in Christ Jesus.
>
> —PHILIPPIANS 4:6–7, NLT

This passage of Scripture seems too simple to be difficult, but it was, because I failed at first to get the part about not worrying. I had not yet given everything over to Him. Therefore, His overwhelming peace eluded me.

You see, you can never worry enough to fix anything. And you can never qualify yourself, no matter how hard you work to be good enough, strong enough, gorgeous enough—*whatever* enough. Looking back over my journey of trying to please others and failing at it again and again, I now see that what I really craved was acceptance. But that comes only by first accepting Jesus' saving grace. Once I did that, His acceptance gave me a totally new identity and set me on a positive track for my future.

To know God's peace, we must accept who God made us to be and embrace the idea that we were beautifully and wonderfully made. Isn't it amazing how other people can see the greatness in us long before we do? That's because we haven't taken an honest, objective look at the vessel God created. He never took the time to make a nobody. He made everybody special in some way. He knows our true identities because He created us.

Once you truly recognize the *you* whom God created, you must choose to accept His version of your identity. I think that means you can't ignore what you dislike about yourself and hope it will go away. We all play that game. We look in the mirror and despise the parts we see as being imperfect. It might be a strong and dominant nose, like mine, or hair that never has a good day or being ten inches taller than anyone else in the family. Whatever it is, *God made it.*

At the same time, the God who never makes a mistake is in the business of change. We all are going through His process of becoming the best possible version of ourselves, which is the version He created. His work is mistake proof. The only mistakes happen when we refuse to let Him rule and reign over our very existence. God cannot bless a mess. What I mean is that He cannot bless who we pretend to be, because He knows our true identities.

If I asked you to describe yourself in one word, what would it be? *Unqualified, hurting, overwhelmed, gifted, disappointed, lacking, weak, strong, stupid, smart*? You see, when your emotions rule, your mind has to work overtime. But that doesn't mean it is telling you the truth. This may come as a shock, but you and I are not necessarily honest with ourselves. Jeremiah made that crystal clear:

> The human heart is the most deceitful of all things, and desperately wicked. Who really knows how bad it is? But I, the LORD, search all hearts and examine

secret motives. I give all people their due rewards, according to what their actions deserve.

—JEREMIAH 17:9–10, NLT

If you are not honest with yourself, how can you be honest with others? You can't. If you want to move forward when your emotions are working overtime, you have to learn to speak the truth to yourself. Remember that "death and life are in the power of the tongue, and those who love it will eat its fruit" (Prov. 18:21). In other words, you get to live out whatever you speak into your own life.

Remember that everything in your life has a season. You are continually undergoing change. Remind yourself that even in the worst of times, your current situation is temporary. That is one way to overcome the challenges that tear so many people apart. You don't have to stay stuck. You don't have to be ruled by your emotions. You can choose to move from one challenge to the next and enjoy your journey. You can choose to set aside other people's negativity (it isn't worth the worry anyway) and be thankful for today.

Testimony

Never in my wildest dreams did I ever think that God would use a lady who has an inbuilt amplifier attached to her vocal cords to help me through the toughest season of my life. She's been shouting at me through my TV screen for over a month now. And what a change it's made in my life. She's like all my favorite preachers packaged in one very unique and extremely powerful individual.

Real Talk Kim, thank you for going through hell and coming out on fire! You have had an eternal impact on this man's life and pushed me to look beyond the current circumstances and pursue God! And I know I'm not the only one who'd confirm this. Thank you so much.

–D

Testimony

Back in 2009 I received a prophecy, and my pastor said that God spoke that I would heal the hearts of many women and I would be a speaker among women one day. He also said that I would have a prophetic word that would shake the nations one day. I was sexually abused for years by my uncle and was in and out of bad relationships and drugs, and I left a good home to live with whomever. I lost myself, even after receiving my prophecy. I have not done a whole lot with my life since then. But when my mom shared one of Pastor Kim's videos, I watched it and immediately felt a shift in my spirit.

That was almost three weeks ago, and my entire household has changed. I am back to writing my book and creating my women's ministry and I believe that back in 2013 when God moved my mom and dad from LaGrange, Georgia, to Fayetteville, Georgia, that this was the reason—so that our family's paths would cross and we would meet Pastor Kim. My parents attend church every Sunday. And my husband and I and two of our three children attended for the first time last week. We love it! My sweet daughter is only six, and she loves Pastor Kim so much that she watches her on *Live at Nine* with me, and she watches her YouTube channel when she goes to bed. We have been blessed by Pastor Kim and I know the purpose and the blessings will continue!

—K

Today's Declaration

Lord, today I decree and declare freedom from the chains of my past. I let go of all hurts, habits, and hang-ups that have caused me to misunderstand my purpose. I now realize that I haven't lost the person You meant me to be. But I am free to lose whatever has blocked me from getting to the me You intended. I decree freedom in my present and my future. Father, Your Word says that whatever I "loose on earth will be loosed in heaven" (Matt. 18:18). *Thank You for the guidance of Your Spirit, the angels who respond to Your Word, and the perfect peace You have invited me to enjoy.*

CHAPTER 2

Afraid to Move Forward

FEAR CAN AND will paralyze you. Left unchecked, it will keep you from moving toward your purpose and destiny. And it is absolutely debilitating, both mentally and physically. Fear is not a new problem. It first showed up in Genesis chapter 3. It is not overtly stated in the text, but why else would Adam and Eve have disobeyed God's command? FEAR—false evidence appearing real.

If you allow it, fear will become progressive. It begins in your mind but can take residence in every area of your life. To combat it, you have to be equipped with God's Word.

What Are You So Afraid Of?

Fear is a real thing, but it did not come from God. "God has not given us a spirit of fear, but of power and of love and of a sound mind" (2 Tim. 1:7). If you let it, fear will rob you of all three. There is an answer for fear, however, and it isn't courage:

> There is no fear in love. But perfect love drives out fear, because fear has to do with punishment. The one who fears is not made perfect in love.
>
> —1 JOHN 4:18, NIV

The enemy comes to steal, kill, and destroy. (See John 10:10.) He will use every available method to achieve his goal, including fear, which is nothing more than faith that has been perverted. Fear is the opposite of all that God has for you. God's plan is to give you "a future and a hope" (Jer. 29:11). But fear will make you doubt God's plan and risk missing the future He has for you. That's why it is so important to renew your mind with His Word and spend time in His presence and in prayer. Prayer isn't some old-fashioned, obsolete means of communicating with God. It is the foundation of your relationship with the Father, the Son, and the Holy Spirit.

Whether I am traveling or relaxing on my deck, two of my favorite things are prayer and worship. Spending time in God's presence gives me the strength and courage to do all that He has purposed for me to do. I know that "I can do *everything* through Christ, who gives me strength" (Phil. 4:13, NLT). I stress this often because it is essential in overcoming the fear that can attack any area of life. We fear lack and provision. We fear life and death. We fear sickness and health. We fear rejection, abandonment, and making mistakes. When bad things happen, we tend to wallow in our pain rather than set a new course. Our minds have a way of making bad situations

God will wreck your plans before they wreck your life.

bigger and more devastating than they really are. Then we're tempted to do things we know we shouldn't.

You don't need another sermon, prophetic word, or conference. Just become the change you want to experience. God has given you a chain-breaking anointing. Even if you feel like a turtle stuck in peanut butter, you can decide to get up and move forward. The decision is yours to make, and no one can do it for you. I know you're up against some things, and some of them might be really tough. Nobody goes unopposed in this life. Everybody has some kind of negative force trying to hold him or her back. But remember, God will wreck your plans before they wreck your life.

Fear is a devourer. In our down times, we wonder why we can't get ahead, why we can't succeed in business, why we can't make a marriage work, why we can't control our temper or break an addiction. When we are fearful, these whys create cycles that keep us depressed and punishing ourselves over and over for past mistakes. What we need is to become aware of what we are doing to ourselves and then deal with the real culprit.

You've heard the voices that continually play in your head. They say, "You'll never make it. You have no right to succeed. You have failed too many times. You were not created to have a happy marriage." You don't have to fear those voices; just come at them with the truth.

Are you getting this? I always say that if you have not succeeded, your season isn't over. For a long time, I wasn't succeeding. I had to learn to become a chain breaker in my own life. Now that enables me to assist you in breaking your chains. But none of that could have happened until I told those negative voices to shut up and get out of my life. Now, by telling you my story, I am proclaiming the victory some people said was impossible.

Power of Past and Future

There is power in your past. To understand it, you need to be aware of the evil forces that keep you stuck in your circumstances. We call them generational curses—family issues that have been passed down through your ancestral lines. Alcoholism, adultery, and depression are just a few examples.

In a seminar about the children of alcoholic parents, I learned that the genes of alcoholic predecessors can make you more susceptible to alcoholism. You may have friends who can enjoy a cocktail now and then. However, if there's a generational curse in your family tree, you might be the one whose body is prone to craving the substance and the behavior. It changes your life because you need to drink every day just to get along.

If you have not succeeded, your season isn't over.

God created families as a beautiful extension of His image. However, we live in a fallen world and are born in sin. Dysfunction comes naturally to us, which is why we need to live in forgiveness. It's important for us to recognize any sinful patterns passed down through our family lines so we can break them and establish a biblical model for the next generation to follow. We can train up our children in the way they should go. Then, as Proverbs 22:6 tells us, they will not depart from it when they get old.

The good news is that the same power that raised Jesus Christ from the dead lives within you. It's true that you cannot change on your own, but through the Holy Spirit you have the power that brings change and will take you into your future, even when you can't see one on the horizon. You were not created to live in bondage to shame, loneliness, negative words, or pain, and none of it has to be permanent.

I can say this confidently as one who kept trying to measure up and kept missing the mark. I finally learned that the circumstances I thought were permanent would change if I allowed God to work in me. God plus me (or you) is a majority!

Isn't it amazing, when life has you paralyzed and stuck in the past, that God can turn everything around in an instant? He can! But sometimes you have to move beyond what you've known to gain the victory. Is it worth it? Yes. Ask the woman in Luke 13 who had been bent over and unable to stand erect for eighteen long years. No one had an answer for her suffering. I'm guessing that by the time she met Jesus, she had lived in fear long enough to be ready for change. It so happened that Jesus saw her on the Sabbath. Every Jew knew that the law forbade doing almost anything but resting on that day. But notice what occurred and how Jesus rebuked the hypocritical leaders:

> When Jesus saw her, He called her to Him and said to her, "Woman, you are loosed from your infirmity." And He laid His hands on her, and immediately she was made straight, and glorified God. But the ruler of the synagogue answered with indignation, because Jesus had healed on the Sabbath; and he said to the crowd, "There are six days on which men ought to work; therefore come and be healed on them, and not on the Sabbath day." The Lord then answered him and said, "Hypocrite! Does not each one of you

> on the Sabbath loose his ox or donkey from the stall, and lead it away to water it? *So ought not this woman, being a daughter of Abraham, whom Satan has bound—think of it—for eighteen years, be loosed from this bond on the Sabbath?"*
>
> —Luke 13:12–16

This woman was unable to move forward in her condition. She had been bent over too long. But Jesus called out to her, on the Sabbath. Do you think she was afraid when the Jewish leader grumbled and criticized Jesus for speaking over her condition? Did she even care? Or was she just thankful that she was finally free?

Jesus let everyone know that she was bound in her situation. That should speak to us right now. Many of us go through life bound by different situations. But what would you do if you knew that one word from Jesus would change everything? Would the critics matter? Would you still be filled with fear? Or would you take your only chance to live a normal life? This is all so profound yet so simple: the same Jesus who stood up amid all the judgmentalism in the first century is still doing miracles today!

When your pain gets so bad that you are ready for change at any cost, you will see change.

When Jesus spoke freedom over that bound woman, she was healed *instantly*. I witness things like that every week. Chains are broken in people's lives, even when generational curses have been operating for decades. Chains of sickness, depression, and even discouragement are broken when people refuse to be ruled by fear any longer. The evidence of their chains might not be as visible as what bound the woman in Luke 13, but their chains are just as disruptive to their lives.

You were not created to go through life broken by limitations. When your pain gets so bad that you are ready for change at any cost, you will see change. Your faith will connect with His Spirit, and change will come. But that freedom starts in your mind. That's where the power of your future is ignited.

During my struggle for freedom, I went through a divorce while caring for my two little boys who were scarred by family disruption. Many days, it was easier to lay in bed with the covers pulled over my head than to attempt to walk through the day. I knew that depression was a generational curse in my family. I had watched my grandmother battle the dreaded affliction for many years. I could easily have accepted that fate and allowed it to keep me bound. Or I could make up my mind to see change in my life. I made the better decision, but I did not make it overnight.

One day, after months of seeing me submit to my brokenness, my brother walked into my bedroom and told me it was time for me to get up, take a bath, and find a job.

"What?" I wondered. "How could he dare speak so harshly? Doesn't he know that I am going through a broken marriage and I've lost everything?"

It was true. Everything was gone—my business, my home, and my friends. Fear kept me locked up in my room, covered up, not wanting to face life or those who were judging me harshly. Yes, I had made many mistakes and wouldn't even listen to counsel. That's why I was too broken to know how to make the next move.

Was I crippled inside? Absolutely!

Seventeen years before that day, my dad had driven me around the I-285 loop of Atlanta for several hours while trying to dissuade me from jumping into a marriage that wasn't ordained by God. I listened and then did exactly what he counseled against. Within a month of getting married, I was pregnant with my first son. I already knew the marriage was a mistake, but I also knew I would do whatever I could to keep it together.

As my situation went from bad to worse, I wondered why I was the only one in my family who couldn't keep a marriage together. I couldn't see the power of my past decisions. I couldn't see a better future for myself either. But that didn't mean that none existed.

The Hard Way and God's Way

Did I mention that this was my second marriage and I was only twenty years old? (I told you I did not do well with counsel!) I was one of those people who would learn only through experience. Why, oh why, did I not follow wise instruction?

Anyway, once our first son was born, life got even rockier for my husband and me. Everyone says that communication, sex, and money are the culprits where marriage problems are concerned. Well, we had our share of difficulties in all three areas. Even after working in ministry, nothing changed. Maybe it was even more difficult because I felt like I was living in a fishbowl.

Our marriage was like the television show *Big Brother*, in which life plays out on the screen. My second husband and I tried to portray the perfect family. We looked really good and played our parts well on the outside. Behind closed doors, we were anything but perfect. On the inside, we were messed up. I lived in such fear—fear that others would discover how broken we were, fear that I would end up alone, fear that my boys would be scarred beyond repair.

Fear of an unknown future can cripple you more than you might imagine. Most of your fears never materialize, yet they can keep you bound. Looking back, I remember expecting the worst. My faith in everything turning out badly was really strong. On the bright side, however, my boys turned out great. Somehow, God covered them with grace and protected their little hearts from devastation. Another great outcome of all that brokenness is that I finally allowed God to work *in* me so He could work *through* me. Honestly, that is why I am so determined to spend every waking hour building up others and helping them to break out of their prisons and rediscover their purpose.

I know now that the answer to breaking the chains in our lives is to get in agreement with God. It is up to us to set a new standard, not only for our lives, but also for generations to come. You see, the decisions we make today will affect our children and grandchildren. We can defy the odds on their behalf. We can invite change to come by moving forward in spite of our fear.

That's exactly what the Israelites had to do. By the time Moses led this group of about two million out of Egypt, they had already been broken down by the Egyptians' cruelty. They had cried out to God for deliverance, and God sent them Moses.

> Moses told the people, "Don't be afraid. Just stand still and watch the LORD rescue you today. The

> Egyptians you see today will never be seen again. The LORD himself will fight for you. Just stay calm."
>
> —EXODUS 14:13–14, NLT

Can you imagine how the people felt leaving the place where they were enslaved for four hundred years? They knew their exodus was a new beginning, but many unknowns were ahead. Then they saw the dust rising behind them and realized that Pharaoh was leading his army to overtake them. I'm sure an all-consuming fear encompassed them that day. It was likely the greatest trial of their lives up to that point. The Red Sea was in front of them, and a fierce army was coming up in the rear. What could they possibly do?

Have you been there? Did you ever feel so surrounded by life's situations that you couldn't figure a way out? Did it feel like the worst day of your life—a day with no answers and no direction?

That's exactly where the Israelites were when God told them He would fight for them. Still, their fear asked, "But *how* is God going to get us out of this situation? Wouldn't we be better off back in Egypt?"

Do you see how fear works? It goes to the root of your devastation and causes you to lose sight of God's Word. Notice what God said to Moses:

> Why are you crying out to me? Tell the people to get moving! Pick up your staff and raise your hand over the sea. Divide the water so the Israelites can walk through the middle of the sea on dry ground.
>
> —EXODUS 14:15–16, NLT

The Israelites were afraid and even confused. Moses told them that God would fight for them. Then God instructed them to move, right after telling them to stand still and see His glory. God needed to see their faith in motion, so they had to move. It was time for them to take a step of faith, believing that God would take them through.

That's how you get out of your stuck places. You refuse to allow life to take you out, and you keep moving. Even when you feel like you cannot gain traction, just keep moving. With God on your side, you are in the majority. Remember when God instructed Moses to raise his staff over the water? Moses obeyed God, and the water parted.

Moses didn't have a "maybe it will happen" attitude. He simply believed what God said. In certain situations, you have no time for "Maybe you'll get better" or "Maybe that wayward child will come home." Living in the land of maybes is no way to live. If God says it, you can take it to the bank and deposit it. It *will* happen.

Change the Narrative

Life is full of situations. Why allow them to limit you? Why not have a new perspective? Say, "I'm not bound; I'm free. I'm not sick; I'm healed. Oh, you think I'll never succeed? Oh yes, I *will* pass that test."

It's time to cast everything in a new light. It's a matter of changing the narrative because your words form your world. We serve a living God, not a dead one. We don't have to feed our God the way idols need to be fed. And we don't have to hope that He hears us when we pray. Our God is risen from the dead. He's the only God who resurrected so we could have everlasting life. There were witnesses to His death and witnesses to His empty grave.

> Very early on Sunday morning the women went to the tomb, taking the spices they had prepared. They found that the stone had been rolled away from the entrance. So they went in, but they didn't find the body of the Lord Jesus.
>
> —LUKE 24:1–3, NLT

When these faithful women went to Jesus' tomb with spices to prepare His body for burial, He was already gone. His grave-clothes were thrown aside, but the cloth that had covered His face was neatly folded and placed where His head had lain.

Many people claim that the placement of the napkin has to do with Hebrew tradition:

> The folded napkin had to do with the Master and Servant.... If the master were done eating, he would rise from the table, wipe his fingers, his mouth, and clean his beard, and would wad up that napkin and toss it onto the table.... The wadded napkin meant, "I'm done." But if the master... folded his napkin, and laid it beside his plate, the servant would not dare touch the table, because... the folded napkin meant, *I'm coming back*![1]

Although some scholars disagree with these claims, we know without a doubt that our Lord *is* coming back. He isn't done here yet. That is why we look for His return daily. Meanwhile, His resurrection means you can make up your mind that your situation will change.

But be patient. Just because you have accepted the freedom His resurrection provides doesn't mean that everything will change instantly. It's time to walk out your freedom. That means refusing to believe the false evidence that appears real. Guilt cannot hold you back any longer. Depression, fear of failure, and addiction needn't control your life. Your chains were broken through Christ's work. If you are His, you are in covenant with Him.

I'm sure the woman Jesus miraculously healed in Luke 13 thought her condition was permanent. But Jesus asked a question: "Shouldn't this woman who is a daughter of Abraham be loosed?" (See Luke 13:16.) He was letting the crowd and the disbelievers know that, because the woman was in Abraham's lineage, she had certain rights and privileges. God had entered into a divine covenant with Abraham. In it, He promised that Abraham's descendants would always be His people and He would always be their God (Gen. 17:1–8). Therefore, the woman in Luke 13, who was a descendant of the promise, should easily have been healed.

The reason I want you to understand this is because you are not just anyone. You are a child of God. You are in covenant with Him. Therefore, Jesus could ask the same question on your behalf: "Should not this son or daughter be free from oppression, addiction, and suffering?" The struggle you face is only temporary. I'm telling you that you have rights, and you need to establish them in your life. Tell every stronghold to be broken in Jesus' name. Then allow Jesus to establish Himself on the throne of your heart.

Almost every day, I ask Jesus to be Lord of my spirit, soul, and body. I then give Him free rein to do whatever He decides is needed in my life. It's a daily prayer because we continually face situations in which we need His spiritual guidance. In myself, I cannot always win, but the psalmist says that in Him "I can run against a troop, by my God I can leap over a wall" (Ps. 18:29).

If God doesn't remove that troop or that obstacle from your path, don't worry. He'll take you over it. We have His promises, but it's up to us to declare that they are ours. As I am writing, I feel that someone is reading this page and deciding that fear will no longer rule his or her every move. It's true: you don't have to be enslaved by your past decisions or people who have put you down. Your life *can* change.

In Acts chapter 12, Peter had been arrested and imprisoned by King Herod. The night before Peter went on trial, he was asleep, chained between two guards. Guards were also stationed outside his cell at two different guard posts. Looking at these facts, we could easily say that there was no possible way for Peter to escape. However, a group of believers was praying for his release. They knew that Herod had decided to put him to death, so they interceded for a miracle.

It would take a miracle! In the middle of the night, an angel showed up, and the chains miraculously fell off Peter's wrists. The cell doors opened, and the angel and Peter walked through both sets of guards!

> When Peter had come to himself, he said, "Now I know for certain that the Lord has sent His angel, and has delivered me from the hand of Herod and from all the expectation of the Jewish people."
>
> —Acts 12:11

Isn't that amazing? Peter had to come to himself to realize what had happened. He then went to the house where everyone was praying and knocked on the door. Finally, someone answered and those in attendance saw Peter alive, standing at the door. Even though they had prayed for hours together, they could not believe their eyes. So, they bombarded Peter with questions. "Why? When? Where? How?" Peter explained what happened and then instructed them to tell the other believers what God had done.

At times in your life, you won't be able to explain the miracle God does—like when you are faced with bankruptcy and your debts are miraculously paid off. Or when you receive a diagnosis of death, but you continue living in good health. Your circumstances may say that your trouble is permanent, nothing will ever change, and there is no hope for improvement. But God's Word says that He has the

Testimony

Real Talk Kim has truly been a blessing in my life. I have been divorced for twenty years. I really thought I had forgiven my ex until Pastor Kim talked about being stuck, and if you've got a pulse, God's got a plan.... I no longer allow my flesh to take over me when dealing with people. I know God has created a new spirit in me and is renewing my mind. Everything that the enemy took, God is giving it back to me. My love, joy, peace, laughing, etc. I learned to own my mess and ask God to forgive me. I have been out of work since March and I lost my house [and] furniture that was in storage. I've not been able to help my son in his last year of college, yet God kept me. Through Pastor Kim, I am learning that He is a real God, and no matter what we are going through, He still loves me. So, I thank God for this woman of God that He has created to be a blessing to all of us that need healing. Oh, by the way, I am praying for my enemies now. I can't wait until they bless me by reading my book. I am writing the vision for God.

–A

last word. Remember, Peter did not even have to speak to those chains for them to come undone.

People were praying for Peter when the angel showed up and the chains fell off. You may have situations in your life—wayward children, a floundering marriage, threatened job loss—that are keeping you up nights. Instead of being afraid to move forward and make decisions about your future or your family, why not give it all to God? You have the right to do this if you have given your life to Him. Instead of allowing crippling circumstances to rob you of your peace and tranquility, imagine what your life would be like without the chains and fear that have limited your potential. Imagine the kind of relationships you will have without the distrust, guilt, and anger that harmed you in the past.

Testimony

I know you probably get messages on top of messages. But I had to share how you pricked my heart in Richmond. I had to come home and completely surrender all, not just the parts of me I wanted to give God. I tend to think I am one tough cookie and forever I said, "It is what it is." But not after Saturday. I thank God for you and the ministry He has put in you. Forever grateful.

–T

Don't be afraid to move forward. It's time to do it. First, you have to give up and let go of the yokes that have bound you mercilessly. No longer will you allow a stronghold to become the norm. No longer will you function in your dysfunction. Fear is not your master anymore.

Today's Declaration

Lord, I decree and declare that it's up to me to receive my freedom. I recognize what has limited my progress, and I declare that it is now being removed. I am ready for favor. I am ready for You to surprise me and break the yokes that have bound me. Today is my day of release from fear! I decree and declare that I now have revelation knowledge to break out of every chain. No longer will I remain stuck in my mess. Instead, I will make my mess a message!

CHAPTER 3

Lost and Alone

STARTING OVER IS never easy—but *keep standing.* The journey can seem long and confusing, and at times you will feel so alone. God has made you unique, and your path toward healing and recovery is one of a kind. That's where you learn to totally rely on Him. At just the right time, He will send someone who can speak life to your seemingly dead situation. Suddenly, you will realize that you are not alone after all. You will say confidently, "God is with me always. He will never leave me."

Starting over means *change.* Some people around you will urge you to cling to what's familiar and comfortable. But God is trying to extract you from the sense of familiarity that "protects" you from the new life He is offering. Instead of trusting Him and moving toward freedom, you have learned (like most of us have) to adjust to the dysfunction that is making your life miserable. It is so easy to get stuck in it!

A change for the better usually includes some kind of separation, which often becomes your key to elevation. You might see all separation as rejection, but sometimes it is God's protection. In the beginning, you might feel lost and alone, but be encouraged by God's message to you: "Don't be afraid, for I am with you. Don't be discouraged, for I am your God. I will strengthen you and help you. I will hold you up with my victorious right hand" (Isa. 41:10, NLT).

The Next Step on Your Journey

Even after you have decided not to let fear rule you anymore, it can be hard to move ahead in victory. So put fear on notice. Let that culprit know that it no longer determines your path. You are walking toward a better life. As you take each step, the following scriptures will help you.

> In all these things we are more than conquerors through Him who loved us.
>
> —ROMANS 8:37

> I can do all things through Christ who strengthens me.
>
> —PHILIPPIANS 4:13

Meditate on those verses. You *can* do all things through Christ who has given you strength. As we saw earlier, you have the same power inside you that raised Him from the dead. If you will remember these two verses of scripture, I believe that you will walk in the victory you already possess. Yes, at times you might feel lost, but you are definitely not alone. You cannot rely on your feelings anyway. You have to learn to trust solely in God and His Word. That means becoming faithful to consistently study His Word and spend time with Him in prayer.

Maybe you have been rejected or even abandoned by those you trusted. That's OK. Let them go. Forgive those who hurt you so that you can move on. Not everybody from your past is assigned to your future. Learn to accept the fact that some people walk out of your life. Let them watch you from a distance. What God has for your future is so much greater than anything you have ever experienced. You don't have to look back.

Starting over is never easy—but keep standing.

I like to say that there are two types of people: those who are attached and those who are assigned. Very rarely will the people in your life fit in both categories. That is perfectly fine. Just remain content and discerning. Sometimes you just have to release people. It is not that they are bad people; they are just not good for you in the current season. You have the power to Ctrl + Alt + Delete. Don't you dare feel guilty about making these choices! You are making them to improve your quality of life. And if people are abusing you—physically, emotionally, or both—it is OK to say goodbye. In fact, doing so will be a gift to you.

Do you remember the story of the invalid at the pool of Bethesda? He was in that condition for thirty-eight long years and became accustomed to waiting for his healing. He had his own little community of friends who were just like him—sick and stuck. They probably sat around discussing their conditions and reminiscing about when they started. I'm sure they encouraged one another at times. Yet none of them was in a position to assist anyone else. We know this is true because when Jesus approached the man, He asked him whether he *wanted* to be made whole. The man replied, "I have no one to help me into the pool when the water is stirred" (John 5:7, NIV).

Sometimes you just have to release people.

This is exactly where so many people are in life. I can personally identify with that, because I allowed life to keep me emotionally crippled for years. If you can relate to what I'm saying, you are in the right place. You might feel incapable or even unworthy of receiving Christ's healing power, but I am here to tell you otherwise. I came to say, "Take up your bed and walk."

Time to Move On

Your season of feeling lost and alone ends today. I have been assigned to encourage you, and I take my assignment seriously. So, I'm telling you that you can endure and overcome any problem or obstacle. I will be right here in these pages cheerleading you toward victory. I know in my knower that this is my life call—to love people back to life. So, work with me now, and let's choose freedom together.

Let's start with a crazy rhetorical question: How do you eat an elephant? The answer is one bite at a time. Walking out your deliverance is no different. It can be overwhelming. You will have moments when you want to throw in the towel. But remember that God is faithful to His promises to deliver you. "The Lord is not slow in keeping his promise, as some understand slowness. Instead he is patient with you, not wanting anyone to perish, but everyone to come to repentance" (2 Pet. 3:9, NIV). I can testify that if you stay the course, you will come out of hell on fire.

I remember when my dad attended a certain prophetic conference. He was at a place in life where he needed an on-time word from God. Many well-known prophets were there, ready to give him a word from the Lord, when this little man from Nigeria stepped up and announced that he also had a word for my dad. The man wasn't on the prophetic team, nor did anyone know him. He was attending the conference just like my dad was. However, he spoke these profound words, which my dad never forgot: "If you throw in the towel, I will throw it back at you."

The comical part of the story is that, of all the prophets who spoke to my dad that day, this short declaration was the one he took to the bank and deposited. He knew this word was from God because he had become very discouraged and was trying to find a way out of doing full-time ministry. He was weary and so tired of working with people who seemed not to get it. Then God sent this man to show my dad that he really was called to the ministry.

If you don't fit in, you're probably doing the right thing.

Don't you see? God will bring people into your life at the right time to give you the direction for your next season. I can tell you that it worked for my dad, because he has been in ministry for more than fifty years.

Look, the devil will try and remind you about all the times you messed up. He will never mention the good times when you dedicated your all to follow God. It's just another tactic he uses to get you off course. He wants to shift your focus to what is unimportant or irrelevant. Instead of taking his bait, do what Paul said:

> Brethren, I do not count myself to have apprehended; but one thing I do, *forgetting* those things which are behind and reaching forward to those things which are ahead, I press toward the goal for the prize of the upward call of God in Christ Jesus.
>
> —PHILIPPIANS 3:13–14

Forget what's behind you. God has! In the midst of your turmoil, keep pursuing your freedom. You are *not* alone. God has warriors who will step forward and cover your back at the most strategic times.

Look Toward Your Future

This is an important season in your life. Everything around you is changing, but most importantly, you are changing. That can be uncomfortable for you and the people around you. Not everyone will accept the person you are becoming. Your job is to keep discouragement from overtaking you. You might be disappointed in your progress or feeling out of place. That's OK. "If you don't fit in, you're probably doing the right thing."[1] God never called you to fit in. He called you to stand out. Don't allow life's challenges to create a new you when God has already created the perfect you.

It's amazing how discouragement can cause you to miss out on the greatest opportunities God gives you. Everyone experiences discouragement. It can come when you're doing your best and no good deed seems to go unpunished. Or it can come when you are at your worst. Sometimes you just need an encouraging word from those closest to you, but they're silent. Whatever the situation, encourage yourself. That's what David did when all seemed lost. (See 1 Samuel 30:6.) If he hadn't, the negative chatter would have thrust him even deeper into the chasm of his despair.

The apostle Paul understood this. When he wrote the Book of Philippians, he had every reason to feel hopeless. According to many scholars, he was under house arrest in Rome.[2] While trusting God for his release (Phil. 2:24), he was aware that he could die for the gospel's sake. When he wrote the passage we just read in Philippians 3:13–14, he was speaking to himself about forgetting the past and reaching forward to what was ahead. He was not living in past mistakes or past judgments. Instead, he was pressing toward the goal the Lord had set before him.

Even at your best, you will sometimes feel isolated and alone—discouraged. You will be tempted to quit being your best when others are barely trying. Rick Ezell talks about how Jeremiah must have felt when God gave him "a harsh message for a rebellious people." Jeremiah obeyed God and was arrested, beaten, and thrown in prison for doing so.[3] In the midst of his troubles, Jeremiah explained his persistence:

> When I speak, the words burst out. "Violence and destruction!" I shout. So these messages from the LORD have made me a household joke. But if I say I'll never mention the LORD or speak in his name, his word burns in my heart like a fire. It's like a fire in

> my bones! I am worn out trying to hold it in! I can't do it!
>
> —JEREMIAH 20:8–9, NLT

Jeremiah "endured physical, emotional, spiritual, and professional anguish."[4] Why, oh why, would people abuse a man of God who was doing the Father's will? Jeremiah's cries remind me of the Lord Jesus' cries when He felt so lost and alone in the Garden of Gethsemane. He knew His death was imminent, and as much as He was fully God, He was also a man who felt alienated. Even His tried-and-true disciples could not stay awake in the garden to pray with Him. (Of course, they did not know the extent of His pain or the consequences ahead or even the judgment that would be pronounced upon Jesus.)

Jesus and Jeremiah remind us that even God's finest servants can get discouraged. Both men were frank in expressing their emotions to God.[5] Both suffered for the sake of people who ignored their warnings. Both served God faithfully, and neither had an idyllic life this side of heaven. Just because you serve God does not mean your life will be idyllic either. In fact, the enemy of this world (the devil) will do everything necessary to disrupt your family, job, church, and life. His goal is to make you lose hope.

How many times have you felt like no one understood you or your pain? If you were to tell your story to a large group of people, you would hear many situations that are similar to your own. It's because we are living in a fallen world. When Adam and Eve chose to eat the wrong fruit in the Garden of Eden, selfishness took the place of godliness. No matter how great other people's lives look from the outside, they have stories of pain and loss, just like you do. No one has it all together.

So, why do so many people continue walking in obedience in spite of the anger and rejection they face?[6] It is because they have kept God's grace in their sights. Because I have gone through my own pain, I can see pain in the faces of people I meet. I thank God daily that, through His grace and mercy, He allowed me to suffer loss and begin this journey of peace.

Each Has Been Called

Each of us is called by God to fulfill a purpose on this earth. No one was chosen to meander through life waiting to be served. Yet when you are called to serve Jesus Christ, struggles will come with the call. Because I was raised in a pastor's family, I've seen the daily challenges up close. Many of my church friends wanted to spend time with me because they thought we had the perfect family life. They never saw the seasons of indecision and even hopelessness my parents faced. But I did. I watched my mom and dad trying to keep our lives together despite the difficulties of ministry.

Many people have asked me whether they should go into ministry, and my answer has changed through the seasons of my life. In my teens, I almost certainly would have said, "No! Don't do it." I wanted to be anything but a preacher's kid. My parents conditioned and trained me to work in ministry. But I would have told anyone I could to run from that life as hard and fast as he or she could. I personally determined to get myself out quickly. At eighteen, I was married in an elaborate wedding and ended up in Mexico. All I wanted was to be on my own with my husband, enjoying a glamorous life in another country. (I certainly did not count the cost.)

I was that girl who worked a full-time job during high school and purchased her own BMW. But in Mexico, I had to drive a little Volkswagen Rabbit. There was another problem: I didn't have a Mexico driver's license, and I couldn't read a word of Spanish. I dug myself a small hole, and it turned into a grave of depression and loneliness. Each day, I would look out the window of our little one-bedroom duplex and see a dirt street filled with garbage. Never had I felt so alone. I would call my parents at three o'clock in the morning, Atlanta time, and they would try to encourage me the best they could from twenty-three hundred miles away.

What was I thinking? Why in the world was I so stupid? Maybe I was just a kid faced with adult decisions I was not ready to handle. I don't know, but I was *stuck*. Have you been there? Have you looked in the mirror and not recognized the face staring back at you?

Every step you take is a step away from where you used to be. Don't make your rut your grave!

That's what happened to me. I had crossed over into a world of darkness like never before. My husband didn't know what to do with me, so he called my parents and asked them to fly me home for a few weeks. I guess he thought that would solve my problem.

It did, for about a minute. Within two weeks, I was missing him. So, we all met in Louisiana, and I returned with him to our little abode in Mexico. We both knew we would never make it there, so we moved back to the States and ended up in Ohio, where he was hired for a position involving weekly travel.

His travel schedule took a toll on our relationship. We never seemed able to come together in harmony and have a normal marriage. Fourteen months after our wedding, we were in divorce court. For years, I never even mentioned this period in my life because it was so long ago and lasted such a short time. Yet my decisions during that brief period changed my life forever and positioned me to plunge into a second marriage on the rebound.

Based on experience, I like to say that every step you take is a step away from where you used to be. Don't make your rut your grave, like I almost did. I kept running from my call and leaped into another marriage without anyone's blessings. Before I turned twenty-one, I had been married twice. There was no one to blame for my troubles but me.

Today, when I rehearse my life, I see how God covered me in spite of my foolishness and my selfishness. It was all about me in those days. One month after I married for the second time, I found out I was pregnant. Screaming, I called my mom, who talked me off the ledge. I'll never forget her words that day. "Baby, you are going to have a child. You will do your best, and we all will be there for you."

That was my problem. I was trying to get away from everyone who had any authority over my life. I thought I could control everything. By the time I realized I was pregnant, I understood that I could not do life alone. Not that I had ever really been all alone. My parents were always sending my husband and me stuff that we needed, including money and even an automobile. Looking back, it's almost comical to see how I tried making adult decisions when I was such an immature brat.

Testimony

A year ago, I lost my grandparents forty-seven days apart, the only ones who showed me love. I'm a single mom of four, but my twenty-five-year-old no longer lives with me. I was in such a very dark place where I hated my life, my situation. I became depressed, suicidal in my own mind, and anxiety hit. I ended up at the hospital and then you came on one of my feeds and the rest is history! I am in a much better place. Finally, I left my ex of five years. I was too broken for him. It hurts and I miss him greatly, but God is my groom now.... I am a queen and I will get and be better every day that passes because God is good. You are one crazy chick, but your bold and loud obedience shook me out of my darkness and back into the light. Oh, how joyful I am for your obedience and love for our Christ! Thank you! Thank you! Thank you! Hope to meet you in heaven because you are taking a lot of us with you.

–K

I wish I could tell you that my life turned around when my sweet baby boy was born, but it didn't. Now I look at my boys, who have become strong young men, and I thank God, knowing that His mercy is the reason they are doing so well today.

Let me get back to the question people ask me about whether they should go into the ministry. Today, I simply say, "Do ministry if you're called." Rick Ezell says it well:

> When you are called, you can't ignore that call. The call comes first from the heart—internal—as a result of the continued drawing from the Holy Spirit. This conviction is as deep within the innermost being of a person.... It marks a person for life. In time the inward call of God

> is reflected outward, as the Christian community confirms it.[7]

I don't know what your calling is. You might be called to run a company or teach children. Maybe you were born to dance or be a writer. The point is to identify your call. Then, come what may, you can turn to God.

During the lost times in my life, I went to God because I didn't know where else to turn. Looking back, I can see how He brought me through every crisis. No one who witnessed my selfish, immature decisions would have believed that I would ever travel the world preaching Jesus. However, now the call of God to love people back to life is confirmed through the Christian community as they invite me to speak at conferences and seminars and on television. It's not an easy role to fill. I could not do it without the internal call and commission of Christ and the external confirmation of His church.[8]

To this day I ask, "Why me?" Then I realize that, at thirty-six years of age, I gave up my plans, which had totally failed, and I began allowing God to conform me to His image. Finally, I see that I am still standing, not because I knew how to work my plan for my life, but because His mercy kept me.

You can decide today to turn your life over to the Creator who chose you for His purpose. Remember that even though God calls and chooses people, many of them do not work with Him. Sometimes it's because they cannot imagine going the distance. But you don't take the journey in one giant step. If you will take even a small step in God's direction, it could make the difference for all eternity.

Testimony

I remember coming across one of your posts on Facebook. I did not know anything about you. I just thought you preached but did not realize how famously known you were. I immediately knew you would be the one to change my life. I had been in a marriage of twenty-three years–no love, no affection, and he just made me feel really ugly. I decided I would go on this journey with you and I began to speak what God says about me. I lost eighty-six pounds and just was on fire. I came to your Level Up Conference, and I have never looked back. My friends thought I was nuts. Even my friends at my job were like, "Who is this person?" But I did not care. You helped me see myself how God sees me. I was free for the first time in my whole life. I have grown, I encourage people every day. I pay my tithes now and give to different ministries. I have a burning desire to serve God and nothing is going to stop me. I wrote a book called *Removing the Blinders*. I'm working on another one now. I have so much I want to do for God. But it all started with one person, a stranger, showing me they loved me, and God loved me, and I could do anything. Thank you for loving me back to life.

–D

Today's Declaration

Lord, I decree and declare that I live for Your approval alone. Help me to need only Your approval. I will not conform to the ways of the world or change who You called me to be in order to please people. Help me to believe and know that You love me just the way I am. I believe that You will heal my brokenness, and the spirit of confusion shall have no power over me. Your name is my strong tower. I run into it and am safe. (See Proverbs 18:10.)

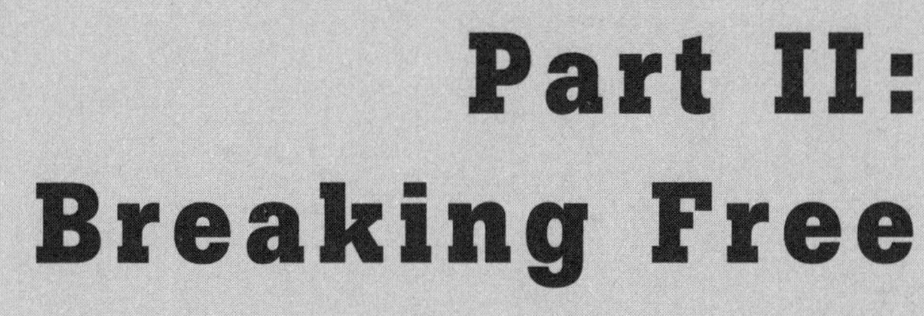

Part II: Breaking Free

CHAPTER 4

Broken but Beautiful

ARE YOU NOT where you thought you would be at this point in your life? Are you not the person you hoped to be by now? It's not the end of the world. Let this awakening launch your first step into a new season. Disappointment over the past does not define your future. Your scars are proof that you have survived. The season behind you may have been your waiting season. Waiting to see the outcome of so many bad decisions. Waiting to see why you were rejected when others were accepted. Waiting to embrace peace in the midst of turmoil.

If you say, "That's me!" I have a word for you.

Don't Waste Your Waiting

Don't waste your waiting. It's easy to be so consumed with whatever happened in the past that you get stuck in it. Instead, you just need to ask, "And?"

"I got fired. *And*?"

"My promotion fell through. *And*?"

"My relationship isn't working out. *And*?"

"They lied about me. *And?*"

"The funding is delayed. *And?*"

The *and* is up to you, but it is time to move forward. Don't wait around to see what life has for you. Make a decision. Do something. Ask yourself, "What's next?" Don't allow would haves, could haves, and should haves to decide your outcomes for you.

Even as I write this, I keep hearing the word *transition*. I see you stuck in cycles of depression, frustration, poverty, and defeat. I pray your eyes are opened to those patterns as you read. I can tell you that when I was (finally) honest with myself and recognized my own cycles, I decided to get off the fast track of loss and to make a change.

The devil should have taken me out when he had the chance because, once I realized that Jesus was directing my life, everything changed. I determined that it was time to quit feeling sorry for myself and my broken life. It was time to do something. Who could have guessed that my journey would look like it does today? I had no idea! Don't get me wrong. I work really hard doing what I love. However, seeing the benefits is worth every effort, every mile, and every day of being away from family.

Your greatest humiliation can set up your greatest elevation.

When you realize that your identity isn't wrapped up in whatever caused your pain (whether a rape, affair, divorce, bankruptcy, etc.), your greatest humiliation can set up your greatest elevation. Why not allow God to give you an extreme makeover? Allow your difficult experiences to reveal your brokenness so you can trade your ashes for beauty.

An Awakening in Action

When something happens that you don't understand or can't control, I believe God knew it was coming and determined beforehand that He would use it to wake you up. It was probably something that you did not plan, something that threw you completely off course and caused so much brokenness that you could not imagine how you would recover.

I recently had such an experience. Because of God's favor, I travel weekly to minister. However, an accident threw me for a loop. Most people who are close to me know that I am a klutz. I certainly don't know what being graceful looks like. So, if someone is going to trip and fall, it will probably be me. Seriously—I have even walked into glass windows while window shopping.

On this particular occasion, I walked hurriedly into my house and tripped over a rug at my back door. Now, I knew ahead of time that I needed to move that rug. Yet, after months of inner conversation about it, the rug was still in the same spot. I had even told others, "We need to get rid of that thing before someone falls and gets hurt."

Little did I know that it would be me. While I fell and grabbed frantically for anything that might save me from going down, my life ran before me like a sped-up movie. I failed to cushion the blow. Instead, I fell facedown on a marble table. I didn't just fall flat. First I hit my chin, then my mouth, and then my nose.

You get the picture.

Something that happened in under thirty seconds affected my whole life, all because a small detail had awaited my attention for months. When I came to myself, I began checking (with some fear) to see what was broken. Of course, my ministry schedule immediately came to mind. I was supposed to speak at a miracle conference in California within two days, and the next week, I was to fly to Australia for four days. What if I couldn't talk? What if I had knocked out my teeth or broken my nose?"

Talk about fear setting in! I was scared silly. Of course, when something like that happens, most of us allow fear to dominate the conversation. The strange thing was that I wasn't really hurting. It was surreal. I wondered, "Did this really happen? Did I really fall and hit my face? What's my next move?"

As I examined my face to see what was fractured or knocked out, I saw no real damage. My nose was still my most dominant feature, and I still had my front teeth. But my entire face had taken a jolt. Because it was late in the evening, I just went to bed and prayed that God would oversee this potentially life-changing episode.

As I prayed, He began telling me that He was going to do something amazing in the next few weeks. However, He needed me to slow down, get off the treadmill, and just listen. You see, I was busy working for God but wasn't taking care of the vessel that He gave me. I might have a call of God on my life that will go with me into eternity, but I have only one body to house that call. It's up to me to take care of myself so I can fulfill God's will.

Sometimes, when everything is going great, you get busy

and forget the One who blessed you. When your new business becomes successful, it's easy to forget your early-morning devotions or late-night Bible reading. Sometimes God will allow your negligence to catch up with you, until you are jolted back into a place where you can hear His voice.

When I awakened the morning after my fall, I looked like I had been in a championship fight and lost the match. My eyes and face were black and blue. Even the inside of my mouth was black. I had a lisp because the jolt had shifted my front tooth. All I could think about was getting better so I could preach at the conference in California. But I had so many questions. "Do I need a root canal? Is my nose fractured? Do I have a concussion?"

The questions would not quit. For two days, I stayed home, afraid that I was going to lose my teeth. I wondered what I would do if I needed my jaw wired shut. I think my fear kept me from seeking medical attention. You know, the old "no news is good news" trick.

Finally, on the second day after the accident, I walked into my mother's house. She gasped when she saw me. I looked like I had cheek implants and had undergone a face-lift. She checked me out and said she thought I would live. However, my assistant asked me to cancel my ministry schedule. It was right to wonder how I could preach in that condition.

As long as you have a pulse, God has a plan.

The reason I share this story is to let you know that everyone goes through times when fear gets in the driver's seat. I know I did! But I will not let fear move in and become a permanent resident. So, I covered my bruises with plenty of foundation and made the trip to California, where I let everyone know about my predicament. I preached with a lisp, *but I preached.*

Those two days of lying in bed waiting for my bruises to heal and my teeth to tighten up were some of the greatest days of my life. I slowed down and listened to the voice of God. Why, I wondered, had I gotten so busy doing the work of ministry that I failed to spend time with the Creator who chose me for the work? It was obvious that the enemy tried to take me out by damaging my mouth. So, I determined that I would become even stronger through this challenge. I would not allow him to shut me up. I would not quit preaching, even if I had to preach with a lisp!

Of course, some waiting was involved with my healing. Waiting is part of life. But don't waste your waiting time by allowing fear to rob you. How many times have you squandered precious moments thinking the worst, only to find out later that everything was going to be all right? Decide that you will not do that again.

After I arrived home from California and went to the dentist, the report was good, for the time being. It kept me going for another week until I could fly to Australia for ministry. Then I returned to the dentist, and he gave me a reality check. I had damaged three front teeth and would need root canals on all three. I gladly sat in the dentist's office for eight hours in one day to begin the process of renovating my mouth. I had no idea that I would end up losing a front tooth and needing veneers and implants—all because I was careless but also because God was teaching me a valuable lesson. I truly learned to just wait on the Lord to renew my strength. There was absolutely nothing I could do but allow my mouth to heal. This girl, who'd always been known to quickly fix anything broken, was now learning that some things cannot be fixed immediately. Patience has not been one of my gifts, and I never allowed anyone to pray for me to have it. You see, I know that Romans 5:3 tells us problems and trials help us to learn patience.

After three months, my journey of mouth renovation was complete. My silly accident cost me thousands of dollars in dental work, but my time of recuperation was the greatest period of renewing my mind and becoming more sensitive to God's voice. I would not allow the expense or inconvenience to overshadow the valuable lesson the Lord gave me through it all. Learning to slow down and hear His voice has been a valuable investment in my ministry. It was worth every dime.

You have been through some crazy times too. Has the enemy muted your life because of them? Have you allowed circumstances (even those you may have caused) to limit your altitude? I'm telling you that God will shift in your favor everything the enemy meant for evil. Your part is to *work with God*. You might lose a battle here or there, but you haven't lost the war.

Remember: when you get overly consumed with what's happened, you can get stuck. I could have lain in my bed and cried a river. I could have missed the miracle conference and the overseas trip. But I didn't. In fact, I preached four times in three days—with a swollen mouth, messed-up gums, and a face full of bruises. On the first night, I even joked to the congregation, "If my tooth falls out, just catch it for me." I simply refused to be muted.

Why not use your disability or misfortune to find the area to which God is calling you? I know I don't want someone who has never experienced pain or loss to tell me how to live for God. My thought is, "Show me your limp. Show me you made it through. Then tell me what you have to say."

Can you hear that? Don't just sit there and allow life to beat you down. Get up and do something about it. As long as you have a pulse, God has a plan.

By the way, at the miracle conference, I was given a prophetic word that the enemy was trying to shut my mouth because of God's words that will flow through me in my next season. Please understand that I am just a carrier of His Spirit and am so humbled that He chose me to love people back to life. He gave me a reason to come through brokenness and be powerful.

Key to Blessings

The key to being blessed is simple: obey God's voice. That means making some clear choices based on His Word. Because I know that God plans to prosper me as I trust Him, I would not let a careless accident derail me, especially when so many people were depending on me to show up.

I have learned that submitting to God's will brings me so many blessings that I cannot contain them. I have also learned that He isn't looking for perfect people to serve Him. He knows that we are full of flaws, and we go through situations that break us. But we can allow those challenges to make us strong. In my worst times, when I have no idea what my next move should be, I search His Word for an answer. The twenty-eighth chapter of Deuteronomy always reassures me that submitting to Him produces His blessings in my life. It will do the same for you.

> If you listen obediently to the Voice of GOD, your God, and heartily obey all his commandments that I command you today, GOD, your God, will place you on high, high above all the nations of the world. All these blessings will come down on you and spread out beyond you because you have responded to the Voice of GOD, your God:
>
> GOD's blessing inside the city, GOD's blessing in the country; GOD's blessing on your children, the crops of your land, the young of your livestock, the calves of your herds, the lambs of your flocks. GOD's blessing on your basket and bread bowl; GOD's blessing in your coming in, GOD's blessing in your going out.
>
> GOD will defeat your enemies who attack you. They'll come at you on one road and run away on seven roads.
>
> GOD will order a blessing on your barns and workplaces; he'll bless you in the land that GOD, your God, is giving you.
>
> GOD will form you as a people holy to him, just as he promised you, if you keep the commandments of GOD, your God, and live the way he has shown you.
>
> All the peoples on Earth will see you living under the Name of GOD and hold you in respectful awe.
>
> GOD will lavish you with good things: children from your womb, offspring from your animals, and crops from your land, the land that GOD promised your ancestors that he would give you. GOD will throw open the doors of his sky vaults and pour rain on your

> land on schedule and bless the work you take in hand. You will lend to many nations but you yourself won't have to take out a loan. GOD will make you the head, not the tail; you'll always be the top dog, never the bottom dog, as you obediently listen to and diligently keep the commands of GOD, your God, that I am commanding you today. Don't swerve an inch to the right or left from the words that I command you today by going off following and worshiping other gods.
>
> —DEUTERONOMY 28:1–14, MSG

I would never have understood this passage had I not been broken, without hope, and then transformed by the grace of God. When my marriage was over, I lost my present and had no idea how to claim a future. My next move was a complete mystery. Up to that point in my life, my parents had always stepped in to save the day. Whatever my husband and I needed, I knew my dad was the first person to call.

Then at the age of thirty-six, I returned to my parents' home with my two young sons, no income, and no hope of finding a job that would provide the type of lifestyle we had previously enjoyed. The independent girl who thought she needed no one now had to accept charity in every form. I was so broken that I could not imagine ever facing the future.

But God!

It would take a book all by itself to outline my journey, but here's the short version: I did nothing to deserve the mercy my parents showed me when I returned home as the mother of two. I could see God's grace in everything my parents did for me. However, they realized they could not save the day.

My marriage was irreparable. The business that sustained our family was lost. Our home would be lost in a bankruptcy.

I certainly didn't see a way out of my crisis. My parents couldn't afford to bail me out one more time—especially not from all that wreckage. It would take a while before I could get past where I was. But eventually, I saw that God really did have a plan for my life. He was just working undercover!

One quick testimony: Two weeks after my parents helped me move into their home in Fayetteville, my mom and I were back in Orlando, where I had lived. I was the president of my own interior design company which, in its best days, was very successful. Of course, when my marriage and life fell apart, so did my business. Now my mom and I returned to Orlando to retrieve some accessories from my garage.

As I did a last walk-through of my beautiful home, my mom placed those accessories in the car. Just then, a man drove by and asked her if the house was for sale. Of course, my mom told him excitedly that we were ready to sell that very day. She knew the bank was starting bankruptcy papers, and she knew I needed a miracle.

The miracle happened! Within three days of meeting that man, we were closing on the house! We lost our equity, but thank God, we were able to sell the property.

Be wise enough to walk away from the nonsense around you.

This was the first of many blessings that I would recognize during my "beautifully broken" journey. Beaten down as I was, I could not appreciate the wonder of it right away. However, my parents knew that God had begun my comeback story. I can't tell you that it happened overnight. My dad thought it would take about a year for me to have some hope. It actually took me about three years to give up and allow God to do a work in me. That's OK. It can take time to be wise enough to walk away from the nonsense around you.

It wasn't easy. Giving up everything and leaving my marriage, my business, and my home was *hard*. I was totally embarrassed when the people who had seen me at my high point now saw me helpless and hopeless. I remember talking to God and letting Him know that everyone was discussing my failures. He gave me a beautiful word, which set the stage for my comeback: He told me to live such a life that the people who judged me would have nothing to talk about.

I had been so hardened by rejection and failure that I needed a new, transformed heart. I know now that God is in the "new heart business." He transforms them. He transformed mine. I had lived in a preacher's home for eighteen years yet never understood mercy. Now, in my shattered state, I saw it. Now, I can honestly say that our God blesses those who allow Him to bless them.

I learned something else too: the way to get free from your less-than mentality is to think of at least one person you can help. Who needs you to get into overflow? Who's counting on your being a source of life? This can happen only when you receive an extreme-overflow makeover. Then you keep getting more of what you give away. As you share with others, I believe there's no way to stop the flow of blessings coming back to you.

I live in awe of how God deliberately blesses me and my family. I know I am not qualified to be ministering to thousands around the world. I am humbled as I receive invitations from some of the greatest churches in this nation. Then I look at Isaiah 66:2:

> My hands have made both heaven and earth; they and everything in them are mine. I, the LORD, have spoken! I will bless those who have humble and contrite hearts, who tremble at my word.
>
> —ISAIAH 66:2, NLT

The girl who was raised in a preacher's home, never missed a Sunday at church, and always participated in Sunday school had never allowed the Word of God to penetrate her being. When I returned to my parents' home, I did not know simple Bible stories. There was no way I could use the Scriptures to fight off thoughts of failure, frustration, and even suicide. I think that is why my recent accident opened me up to such a realization. During my quiet time lying in my bed with my face and mouth swollen and bruised, I went to God's Word, and it comforted me. I realized how much I had matured in the Spirit. I now know that even though I may go through traumatic seasons, I will not allow brokenness to rule me. I have given myself over to God's will so He can overflow through me. You see, overflow is the proof that an extreme makeover has happened.

Never feel guilty for cutting someone out of your life who handed you the scissors.

Change That Makes a Difference

Reflecting back on my journey shows me how much my life has changed. If you ask my former friends and acquaintances whether I'm different, you will hear many examples of how God has totally remade me. It was years before some of my former friends would reenter my life. The time of separation was hard at first but not forever. As former NFL player Trent Shelton says, "Never feel guilty for cutting someone out of your life who handed you the scissors."[1] It might mean a temporary season of loneliness, but God will be your best friend if you let Him.

Reading the blessings in Deuteronomy 28, I can see that I now live in overflow. What may be even more amazing is that I don't need to compare myself with anyone to feel like I have succeeded. I don't need to check out other ministries to believe that I am blessed. And although I am blessed in every way, I don't use finances or my home or a nice car as examples of my blessings. To me, blessing is being able to sleep at night without the "help" of alcohol. It's flying from city to city and never fearing a crash. It's knowing that in the midst of my family's greatest crisis (my dad has advanced Alzheimer's), God has a plan.

Testimony

I want to say thank you for just being that light to my life because I have been so down and so dark inside that you make me know that there is hope. I just thank you for all the prayers you pray every night. I feel like there is hope for me, and all the depression and anxiety I don't feel anymore. I love you so much and I thank you. You're a true queen.

–C

God doesn't want to bless you with just a little bit. He wants to pour overflow blessings throughout every area of your life. He is just waiting on you to begin walking in agreement with Him.

Testimony

When I first started listening to you, it was in 2015. I was a new mom and a single one at that. My daughter and I lived with my mom in her camper. I was also struggling with postpartum depression. Every day, I had horrible thoughts of suicide. I was there alone most days because my mom was a teacher and was gone almost twelve hours a day. I was in such a dark place, and your videos began to cheer me up. I would pray daily to God so I wouldn't hurt my child or myself. I was so scared because the enemy would tell me, "Go ahead. Do it. You've already killed one baby–why not another!" Because you see, in 2007, I had an abortion. No one in my family knows about it yet. I did tell my church family a couple of months ago as part of my testimony. But watching your positive videos helped me to even tell them and get it off my chest. Like the woman with the issue of blood, I carried that for twelve years. Now, I have begun to write my testimony. I never thought I'd ever write a book, but I feel like my story could help at least one woman and one child be saved. You've said so many times on *Live at Nine* that there are people who will write books, and I believe I am one. Thank you for your positive outlook! I needed someone real in my life. It has helped me see that in my transparency with my testimony, maybe someone else can be set free.

–A

Today's Declaration

Lord, I decree and declare that I am blessed coming in and going out. I am blessed in the city and the country. Lord, I am allowing You to use my experiences to create in me a clean heart, a pure mind, and a right spirit. I know You have a plan for me, and I will work that plan. I declare by faith that You will supply all my needs spiritually, financially, physically, and emotionally and that, in every aspect of my life, I will yield abundant fruit.

CHAPTER 5

Bigger Than My Circumstances

LIFE IS FICKLE. It doesn't matter how well you started or whether you were voted most likely to succeed. Life can shift in a moment, causing feelings of inadequacy and fear. Even so, you are not your mistakes or what has happened to you. You are bigger than your circumstances.

A favorite scripture that I quote often is Romans 8:28: "We know that all things work together for good to those who love God, to those who are the called according to His purpose." Because we all experience ups and downs, one of my favorite sayings is "Life just happens." It can seem as though we spend more time being down than being up. All of us have felt like quitting in the face of challenges so tough that we can't figure a way out. If you're like me, you look back and wonder how you allowed your circumstances to determine your path for so long.

You might feel like you have lost a lot more than you have gained. Nobody means for it to go that way. You had goals. You had a vision board. Yet where you are right now was absolutely not part of your plan. You might even sit in church on

Sunday and wonder whether being there is a waste of your time. Maybe you're thinking that God has forgotten you or turned down the volume on your prayers.

I can assure you that He hasn't! The Scriptures state clearly that God knows your name and address. (See Psalm 139.) He has very clear ideas about your life, and He says so: "I know the thoughts that I think toward you, says the LORD, thoughts of peace and not of evil, to give you a future and a hope" (Jer. 29:11).

You might think God's promise is for everyone but you. Don't you know the enemy tells you that to dispel your faith? It's easy to look through the eyes of self-pity and tell yourself that no one cares. But you have no earthly idea how many people have put you on the top of their prayer lists. You have no clue who focused on you and your needs as they sought God today.

You are not your mistakes or what has happened to you. You are bigger than your circumstances.

Let me use my life as an example of what I'm saying. God was thinking of me throughout my years of rebellion, when I wanted to forget that I was raised as a preacher's kid. I wondered why I couldn't be like my friends whose parents hung out on Sunday and didn't worry about all those Christians who, in my opinion, weren't special anyway. I could hardly wait to grow up, leave home, and do my own thing. I wanted to show the world how independent and strong I could be. Then I could go to church on Sunday if I felt like it, or I could go to the beach instead. I didn't see what difference it made because I'd never understood what involving God in my everyday life would do.

Against my wishes, my mom would always sit my brother and me down at bedtime and pray with us. My dad was usually out leading home group meetings, as my parents were church planters and starting a new church. I did not understand the importance of my mom being at home with us and establishing a godly family life while my dad worked outside the home for the kingdom of God. I look back now and realize how much I resented our family's not looking like every other family on our street. Of course, I get it now. If my family had been just any family, my parents would not have known how to fight in the Spirit for my very life as I rebelled against all that we had.

There's Grace for That

I had no idea that I was setting myself up for rejection, loneliness, and even trauma by rejecting the source of the peace that encompassed our home. Today, I am so thankful for the strength that kept my parents fighting for my future, even when I had decided to do life my own way. I did not realize that I would initiate a landslide of events that, apart from the grace of God, could have taken me out.

Please understand that you are never in your life situation alone. Even when you feel abandoned and betrayed, God is with you. He *never* leaves nor forsakes you. That is probably the most important thought I can leave with you! Of course, everyone's challenges are different. As you're reading this chapter, you might be thinking, "Kimberly doesn't understand my situation."

You are right. I cannot know all that you are going through. You might think I have no clue about the mess you're facing at home, the grief you catch at work, or the people at church who do nothing but judge every move you make. But I can tell you that even your toughest situations will make you better if you let them.

You probably want to know how that's even possible. I'll let the apostle Paul explain:

> He [Jesus] said to me, "My grace is sufficient for you, for My strength is made perfect in weakness." Therefore most gladly I will rather boast in my infirmities, that the power of Christ may rest upon me.
>
> —2 CORINTHIANS 12:9

Paul was praying about a thorn in the flesh that troubled him. No one really knows what the situation was, but most scholars feel that it was God's way of helping Paul to stay humble. Paul called the thorn a "messenger of Satan" that tormented him and kept him from becoming proud. (See 2 Corinthians 12:7.) I can understand how Paul might have been tempted by pride. Scholars estimate that he wrote anywhere from a third to almost half of the New Testament books! But God certainly would have wanted His apostle to stay humble so he could hear His voice.

The apostle Peter described godly humility saying, "Humble yourselves under the mighty hand of God, that He may exalt you in due time" (1 Pet. 5:6). Those who do this are exalted—not by themselves but by God. Paul's thorn kept him human in the eyes of those who followed him. He could have tried to outshine even Jesus Christ. The

Savior had already been crucified and resurrected, but Paul was there in the midst of the people. You know how the crowds love to find that current star, that special leader, the influencer who will change their lives. That's how cults are formed. People often take their eyes off Jesus Christ and rely on human messengers to give them revelation.

In my daily interactions with people, I ask the Lord to help me remain transparent. I share my life struggles so they can be examples to those who are looking for answers. I want them to see that I find my answers on my knees. It's not about giving glory to a man or woman. It's about knowing the One who has a plan and who works that plan for you.

Many more people might have received Paul's preaching if everything had gone well for him. But the thorn in his flesh showed people that he was a man who struggled just like they did.

The fainthearted could not survive under such a leader. You're reading this book because you are not fainthearted. You are looking for answers to get through your challenges. Eventually, you will realize that if Paul did it, so can you. And if I can do it, so can you. You might be facing one trial after another, but your purpose is still bigger than all of that.

Look at what Paul wrote about his struggles: "A thorn in the flesh was given to me, a messenger of Satan *to buffet me,* lest I be exalted above measure" (2 Cor. 12:7). Please understand that Paul used the word *buffet* to show that he was struck repeatedly, like a shoreline beaten by one crashing wave after another. Have you ever gotten through one challenge and breathed a sigh of relief only to get a bad diagnosis from the doctor or have some other crisis erupt in your family? Personally, I don't think Paul's infirmity was sickness. I think it was more about the persistent spiritual opposition he faced. I'm sure he wanted the Lord to show Him how to be delivered from the torment that plagued him. Scripture says he went to God three times for an answer. (See verse 8.)

Haven't you been there? You fasted, prayed, asked others for help, and still saw no way out. I've been in a place where I walked the floor and cried out to God for help with my marriage, my business, my finances. Looking back, I know those challenges served a purpose. Had I not gotten uncomfortable in my pain, I would not have reached out to God. He was giving me strength even when trials were trying to tear me apart. It wasn't just a battle for my marriage or business; it was a battle for my life. The enemy did not want me to be where I am today. He did not want me to see the strength I would gain when I allowed Jesus Christ to be Lord of my life.

When Paul asked the Lord for deliverance, the Lord simply said that His grace was sufficient. Thank you, apostle Paul, for writing about your troubles so I would learn to acquire strength by passing life's tests. Thank you for revealing that you dealt with thorns in the flesh just like I do. Knowing this makes you so much more human to me. And it makes me a better person.

It's Up to You

Let me assure you right now that you will move from brokenness to beautiful if you choose to *stand*. God has given you a promise to help you: "You are of God, little children, and have overcome them, because He who is in you is greater than he who is in the world" (1 John 4:4). Jesus in you is greater than any trial or tribulation that tries to devour you. It is up to you to believe it.

I am a witness that you cannot change your life on your own. When I was in a failing marriage, I did everything I knew to make things right. That doesn't mean my ex-husband gets all the blame. Throughout my life, I had tried to prove my worth to everyone in my world and to show them that I was qualified to take the helm of my ship. I did not realize that giving my life to God could turn everything around. So, no, I wasn't able to save my marriage. And yes, it does take both spouses working together to make it work. In any case, that trial took its toll. But six years later, I met an amazing man who loves God more than he loves me. He allows me to see his manhood by being in his Bible daily. Humility looks really good on him.

I need to tell you that getting your life together and walking out God's plans for you doesn't mean you won't experience negative reactions from people in your circle. Not everybody celebrates when you go from loss to victory. The enemy surely doesn't want you blessed, so he'll send whatever distractions he can find to create a detour on your journey. However, your call from God is bigger than your circumstances.

A great example is Joseph, the young Hebrew who became second in command to the Egyptian pharaoh. When Joseph was only seventeen, he was already dreaming dreams of greatness and telling his brothers how he would be their leader someday. Of course, his brothers were green with envy! Joseph was their younger brother and their father's "pet." So, they decided to get rid of him and tell their dad he was killed by wild animals.

Their plot meant Joseph would be sold to merchants who were en route to Egypt. They in turn sold Joseph to a powerful Egyptian named Potiphar. Of course, Joseph was a slave in Potiphar's house, but he was gifted and chosen by God to become a leader anyway. After being falsely accused by Potiphar's wife and thrown into prison, Joseph was promoted again and given responsibility in the prison.

The dreams that first caused Joseph to be rejected and sold into slavery ultimately helped him find his way into Pharaoh's palace. It's amazing! The enemy tried to eliminate Joseph's influence, but God elevated him. Years later, when his brothers came to Egypt begging for food during a terrible famine, they did not recognize Joseph. But he recognized them and saved his entire family.

The great revelation of this story is that Joseph discerned God's hand in placing him in Egypt for a specific purpose. When his brothers finally recognized him, they were sure that he would retaliate against them, so they begged for mercy. Of course, Joseph told them that what they had meant for evil, God meant for good. (See Genesis 50:20.) He never intended to be unmerciful toward his brothers, because he had gone from broken to beautiful. This outstanding young man turned negative events into positives. I think Isaiah 54:17 perfectly describes Joseph's story:

> "No weapon formed against you shall prosper, and every tongue which rises against you in judgment you shall condemn. This is the heritage of the servants of the LORD, and their righteousness is from Me," says the LORD.

Take this scripture to the bank and deposit it! When people or situations come against you, you can stand squarely on your feet and tell the enemy that he has no right harassing you.

I see many people who allow the enemy to beat them up. They just lie down and surrender. There was a time when I did the same thing. However, when I realized that it was my job to stand, I became a mighty warrior in the Spirit. Isaiah 54:17 says that this is our heritage as servants of the Lord. Our righteousness comes from Him. We're not righteous by our own might. His Word promises that He will stand with us. He makes us righteous. Our responsibility is to yield and allow Him to be Lord. It sure makes the Christian life a whole lot easier.

Stand Firm

Your obligation is to make sure that you don't allow distractions to take you out. Remember, it's not in your power to walk this walk alone. A favorite scripture passage on which I depend daily says, "The steps of a good man are ordered by the LORD, and He delights in his way. Though he fall, he shall not be utterly cast down; for the LORD upholds him with His hand" (Ps. 37:23–24).

Please understand that God has His eye on you. He has already ordered your steps for today, tomorrow, and the next day. He promises that, even if you fall (which you will), you will not be cast down. In other words, He's got you. When you really and truly believe it, you can serve the Lord even though you are imperfect and sometimes mess up. The enemy wants you to stumble in the fear that God will not forgive your brokenness. But God knew about it from the beginning. That's why He made a way for you to get back on your feet and keep going. There *is* a way out of your mess!

In the meantime, you cannot afford to take your eyes off the prize, which is the kingdom of God. Even if you live seventy or eighty years on this earth, it's only a blip on the screen of your life, because you will live eternally after you die. Remember that "what we suffer now is nothing compared to the glory he will reveal to us later" (Rom. 8:18, NLT).

That's why I have decided to keep standing.

You might not understand why you face so many pitfalls in life. Why were you given that dreadful diagnosis? Why did the one you loved more than life choose not to love you back? I don't know! But whatever you suffer is nothing compared to the glory that the Lord will reveal to you later. Remember Joseph's story. Even though he was given powerful dreams, he had to accept them by faith. I doubt he imagined that God was positioning him to save his nation. How could he have dreamed of receiving such favor from Pharaoh when no one in his world had ever received such treatment from another nation?

Joseph was one of a kind, and so are you. God never takes time to make a nobody. You are definitely a somebody in His eyes.

God Always Had You

As a baby I traveled with my family as my parents evangelized throughout the United States. My dad was anointed and called to the work. He came from a family of revivalists who ministered in tent revivals and started new churches. It was only natural that my dad followed in their footsteps.

I knew about full-time ministry only because my family did it fifty-two weeks out of the year. I never could have dreamed that I was called by God to evangelize as my parents and my dad's family had done. My brother chose to become a pastor in his early twenties, so it was no surprise when he stepped in to pastor the family church. However, this girl had determined early on that she wasn't going down that path. I ventured out from our family covering for eighteen years. I returned broken, needing those who were near and dear to me and my boys. Unlike Joseph, I resisted my family's dreams about picking up the mantle of ministry.

But God had a plan. His Word lets each of us know that we are chosen. The psalmist said it this way: "You saw me before I was born. Every day of my life was recorded in your book. Every moment was laid out before a single day had passed" (Ps. 139:16, NLT).

God knew I would try early in life to do it my way. He knew I would try to do it on my own. He knew that I would come back broken. And He knew He would be there when I reached out for help. Thank God for His mercy!

So many of the quotes I post on social media come from the

Testimony

My husband of fourteen years left me and my eight-year-old last week. He said he needed a break from me to see if he is still in love with me. I called my friend who is like a mom to me and she told me to find you on Facebook. I am so glad I did. I have learned to move on fast and let God. No pity party for myself but getting up every day for myself, my son, and God. I had the best sleep in four years when Kim said, "Give it all to God and don't worry about it." I let God. And I talked to my husband last night and told him I am sorry for all the mean things I've said, and I forgive him even if he did not ask for forgiveness because that is what God wants me to do—to show kindness to confused people. My son and I continue to pray for [my husband]. Thank you, God, for Kim and her ministry to help my son and me in this difficult time.

—A

tough situations I created for myself, including the relationships I had with people who were detrimental to my future. So when I fell on my face, lost and broken, the people who had been my mainstay no longer wanted to come along for the ride.

They might laugh at your process, but you will laugh in your promise.

Don't expect those whom God hasn't called to walk beside you to stay with you when the going gets rough. They might laugh at your process, but you will laugh in your promise. Understand that joy can come in every area of your life when you give your life entirely to Jesus Christ.

The call on your life is so much bigger than your circumstances, but it's up to you to choose your path. God will work with you when you are ready. Why not decide today that you are done with going it alone? Why not surrender and be free?

Today's Declaration

Lord, I decree and declare that I am walking in a spirit of boldness. I have a peaceful spirit and sound mind. I am powerful, anointed, and chosen. I give You my entire being to use as You please. I am excited to be a yielded vessel as You lead me into a victorious life. I thank You for the blessing of abundance in my life and for generations to come, in Jesus' name.

CHAPTER 6

God Has a Plan

WHEN YOUR SITUATION seems out of control, it's important to realize that life could be much worse. It's worth repeating: as long as you have a pulse, God has a plan that is greater than whatever you are experiencing right now and greater than your past. Get that truth settled in your heart, and your situation will change.

A Bible story that really drives this home for me is the one about the Samaritan woman who met Jesus at the well. Scripture says that Jesus had just "left Judea and departed again to Galilee. But He needed to go through Samaria" (John 4:3–4). What an awesome statement that is! Jesus didn't need to stop there, but He knew that a certain woman would come to the well, hear His words, and believe them.

The fact that the encounter happened in Samaria is amazing all by itself. Samaritans were despised by the Jews, and even the Samaritans considered this woman an outcast. That is why she came to draw water in the middle of the day. Most people would have gathered in the cool of the day and chatted with their neighbors as they worked. But this woman was living with a man who wasn't her husband. She would not have been welcomed to the conversation. Not only that, but she'd had five husbands before she moved in with her current partner.

This story is so beautiful because it shows the love of God toward us. I can tell you that I had plenty of sins in my life that would compare to what this woman did. Most women would not easily relate to her lifestyle and her series of partners. In fact, women who are extremely popular with men tend not to have a host of women friends. That's because other women do not trust them to be around their husbands. So, I'm sure this Samaritan woman lived a lonely life.

When she came to the well and drew water, it's unlikely that the Samaritan woman paid much attention to the man who was resting there. But then He spoke to her, saying, "Give Me a drink" (John 4:7). The unnamed woman was shocked that a Jewish man would even speak to her, a woman and a Samaritan. She had no idea that He had come for her sake.

But God had a plan for her. It was time for her to come face to face with Jesus Christ. I thank God that He knows my name and confronted me face to face after I suffered severe losses. I thank God that I was able to surrender and let Him take over my life. Isn't it amazing that we can stumble into miracles—that people like you, me, and the Samaritan woman can meet *Jesus*?

The meeting at the well was not accidental, however. Jesus did not stumble onto the scene by chance. It was planned before the woman's birth. God knew all that had happened since. He knew about the bad decisions she'd made, and He knew that she had little support from the people around her. He knew every detail, just as He knows every detail about us:

> O LORD, You have searched me and known me. You know my sitting down and my rising up; You understand my thought afar off. You comprehend my path and my lying down, and are acquainted with all my ways.
>
> —PSALM 139:1–3

Jesus was at the well for a reason. The encounter had been arranged long before the woman made her first bad choice. She was chosen by God for *that* specific time. Once she met Jesus, she would have to choose her path going forward. The Messiah Himself had touched her life. Despite the Samaritans' distrust of Jews, a Jewish man came and told her everything about her life. Not only was He accurate, but He was also not condescending. She soon realized that He was more than just a man, but she tested Him just a little to be sure.

> The woman said to Him, "I know that Messiah is coming" (who is called Christ). "When He comes, He will tell us all things." Jesus said to her, "I who speak to you am He."
>
> —JOHN 4:25–26

Can you picture the woman before she went to the well that day? She left the house feeling (as usual) that her life was a dead-end street. No girlfriends, no future, no children—just one man after another coming into her life. Jesus waited at the well so He could offer her an alternative she could not have imagined. Jesus asked a woman who was thirsting on the inside to give Him water. When she did, He gave her a new lease on life. He quenched her spiritual thirst the way water quenches the natural thirst.

Part of what keeps us from moving past our traumas is the belief that we are stuck in our bondage. However, God always has a plan for our freedom. Jesus assumed the task of delivering a woman who was bound not only by her own actions but also by the opinions of others. Out of all the people in that village, Jesus chose her—someone who had nothing going for her. I believe that is the way our Lord works. He doesn't choose the most capable, the most beautiful, or the smartest. He takes those whose lives are full of distress, those who have failed at every venture, those who have a lifetime of bad choices behind them. Then, in a moment, He changes their direction and gives them a future.

Jesus asked a woman who was thirsting on the inside to give Him water. When she did, He gave her a new lease on life.

Why in the world would anyone throw away such an opportunity? Why would anyone not invest herself in knowing that, even when she falls, she will not be destroyed because Jesus, the God of second chances, loves her? I thank God that this woman believed Jesus that day. Other Samaritans might have resented Him and rejected His words, but this woman ran back to her village and told everyone that the Messiah was at the well! I doubt that everyone jumped on board immediately, but she did not let anyone's opinions deter her.

God is so awesome that He blocks those who try to block you! Can you imagine the disciples' shock when they returned from getting supplies and saw Jesus talking to a Samaritan woman? Yet they kept quiet. What right did they have to determine the Lord's actions anyway? They had seen many miracles and many changed lives. It may have even become routine to them. However, this woman was changed from the inside out because she believed. Then she immediately started the revival in Samaria. She didn't preach a sermon or pressure people to believe what she believed. She simply told them to come and see Jesus for themselves. Jesus didn't need her to promote His message. He *was* the message. Wherever He went, lives were changed.

There is no healing in hiding.

No matter how long you have been doing what you're doing, you can get out of your situation. God always has a plan for you. In Christ, there's always a pathway to beautiful.

Hidden Sins, Hardened Heart

I hear from people all the time whose feet are chained and whose mouths are muzzled by hidden sins. They are trying to figure out the way to freedom. Many are addicted to pain, rejection, or loss. They don't yet realize that God has a plan or that deliverance means freedom. Many of them are so scarred and wounded, so calloused and hard-hearted, because they have hidden their sins as a way to protect themselves from the hurt and rejection of others.

"There is no healing in hiding."[1] When pain and rejection become your norms in life, it's easy to push away the people who want to help you. Maybe you can't yet understand that you don't deserve all the pain you have endured. You think you're a hopeless case and you must hurt others before they hurt you. I get it. Hard times can make you hateful. I was known as a hard-hearted person. I remember lying in bed believing that no one would care if I died and nobody would come to my funeral. Of course, that was not the truth; it was what the enemy was telling me. But I still believed it. Down deep, I knew that my family would be there when I decided to make a change. Of course, the ball was in my court. Nothing would change until I made the choice to *accept change*.

Life's challenges can cause us not only to hide our sins but also to resist compassion. We don't know how to accept the mercy of others until we tear down our walls of resistance and begin to feel and respond to Jesus as the Samaritan woman did at the well. Jesus saw her as a person who needed a friend. Isn't it extraordinary that He didn't send one of His disciples to minister to her? He knew her reputation. He also knew the disciples would have a problem talking with her because of it. Remember, it was against the custom of that day for a man to talk to a woman alone. But a Samaritan woman—especially one with such a questionable reputation—would have been totally off limits.

That did not stop Jesus from being merciful. Nor did it stop the woman from receiving the mercy she desperately needed. I hope that encourages you as much as it does me!

Satan Knows You Have an Assignment

I wonder how many people reading this book have a special assignment from God. Are you one of them? Has He called you to change your world? Then all you need is a visit from Jesus. Yes, hell will give someone special instructions to take you out. That's because the enemy is terrified of what you will do for God when He sets you free. The enemy knows that once you are back on your feet and making a stand, you will have an impact—not just on your street or in your city but also in your nation.

When God says that He'll give you back better than you lost, believe Him. The enemy knew that when I reached the end of myself and submitted to God's purpose for my life, I would jet all over the world for one reason: to love His people back to life. I really cannot describe the fervor and love that lead me day and night to spend time with people. It's especially crazy because I did not even like people until my Damascus Road experience with Jesus Christ. (If you are wondering about this experience, read Acts chapter 9. Paul, who was then called Saul, was headed to Damascus when he encountered Christ and was stricken blind. The experience caused him to become a disciple like no other. I believe that no one in history ever set the church on fire quite the way Paul did. He embraced the spiritual change God offered, he submitted himself to God, and he allowed that submission to dictate his actions for the rest of his life.)

The enemy has lots of strategies for sabotaging your assignment. I mentioned one of them in chapter 2. It involves generational curses in your family line. These are simply demonic assignments that are meant to decimate your family. I am very familiar with the subject because my parents always warned me to steer clear of alcohol. They did this because so many of our family members have been alcoholics. Before my dad's dad became a preacher, he was an alcoholic. Then my dad's brother died from cirrhosis of the liver because he loved anything that included alcohol as an ingredient.

My dad was so serious about this family curse that he attended a seminar for the children of alcoholic parents. Now remember, his dad had been delivered and changed his life at thirty-five. However, he knew that the desire for alcohol was lurking in our genes. My dad's brother always declared that he would quit drinking at age thirty-five, like his dad had done. It did not happen. Instead, he drank until he ended up hospitalized and in a coma at forty-eight. It's so unfair that my cousins had to grow up without their dad even before he passed away. Because their father was so hooked on alcohol, he dropped them off at my granddad's house so he could raise them. I'm not telling you this to make my uncle look bad. I'm sharing our family's story to say you don't have to lose your life to drugs, pornography, sex, or anything else that is driving you to ruin.

There is always hope for us to break out. Because I had allowed so many addictions to govern my life, I was ready at thirty-six to break the generational curses that had been destroying my future. It became my mission to be free of the pain that was passed down and landed on my doorstep because of what I allowed. It was time for me to shut hell up and put an end to Satan's sabotage of my future.

Breaking Generational Curses

To break a generational curse, you must avoid the unhealthy habits that have haunted your family. You cannot entertain those activities and expect to live differently from those who succumbed to them. I know I cannot drink socially and expect to remain the vessel that God has chosen me to be, because I have a tendency to become addicted.

Now, if you ask me whether I have tried alcohol, the answer is *absolutely,* because that's my personality. I have always been the life of every party. If that meant drinking, I thought I could handle it. When my husband drank, I told my mom that I would drink socially with him in order to save our marriage. I was still allowing my insecure personality to determine my actions. Fear drove me to embrace a life that opened the addiction doors I knew were there.

Not all the alcoholism in our family was on my dad's side. Even my mom's dad had a family of alcoholics. My great-granddad spent all his earnings on drink. His children (including my maternal granddad) had to fish in order to feed the family. My granddad's brothers were also alcoholics, and their entire families suffered lack.

My granddad was a drinker when he married my grandmother. However, he didn't realize how strong that little woman could be. After being married only a few weeks, he came home drunk one night and got so sick that he was vomiting. His cries for help fell on deaf ears. My grandmother saw his condition and told him that she would not be cleaning up his mess or assisting him into bed. The next morning, she informed him that she would not stay married to an alcoholic. Her two brothers were abusive alcoholics, and she had resolved that she would rather live alone than suffer as her sisters-in-law and their children had suffered. She was not about to become pregnant and subject her children to the consequences of this dreaded disease.

I know what happened to my granddad doesn't happen to

everyone. He simply gave up drinking because of my grandmother's resolve and never drank again during seventy-seven years of life. He even gave his heart to Jesus and was the first in his family to receive the Holy Spirit. As with the Samaritan woman at the well who helped bring revival to Samaria, my granddad was the first in his family to become a minister. He even built a church in his community that is still being used sixty years later.

I understand why Satan wanted to take me out and entangle me in the partying lifestyle. However, I had a say in the matter. I refused to allow generational alcoholism to be revived in my lineage, so I had to take a stand. You see, when you make a decision to change, you set up favor for your family. You don't have to do it alone either. Not only will loved ones and leaders help you, but God's children have heavenly helpers too. "Are not all angels ministering spirits sent to serve those who will inherit salvation?" (Heb. 1:14, NIV).

All of us have been oblivious at times to what's happening around us. Had I not had the prayers of my family covering me during a tumultuous marriage, I don't know where I'd be today or if I'd be here at all. After a particular rough night, I promised God that I would change my life because He had saved me again. Yet I did not follow through. I believed that a short break in the chaos was a sign that the trouble was over, when it was not. More times than I can remember, angels covered me when I could have easily been taken out. I had no idea that the Lord had spared my life again and again. He did it at least in part because He had called me to reach into hell and pull people out. Now, I refuse to be quiet, because there are people who will listen to the transparent story of my old, hopeless life.

When we awaken to the reality of our personal challenges, we have to make better choices. It was important for me to get away from the craziness of my life and avoid the pitfalls of alcoholism, not only because I wanted to live, but also because I wanted my boys to have a future. If all they saw were substance use and marriage crises, how could I expect them to become more than what they had seen?

You see, our lives are not only about us but also about others. Every life matters because it was bought with a price. Isaiah tells the beautiful prophetic story when he describes the Lord being beaten and crucified for us:

> But He was wounded for our transgressions, He was bruised for our iniquities; the chastisement for our peace was upon Him, and by His stripes we are healed. All we like sheep have gone astray;

Testimony

When I felt like giving up, Real Talk Kim loved me back to life. When I felt like no one cared or loved me, Real Talk Kim has loved me through *Live at Nine* and the Inner Circle. I always thought someone had to be physically present to be in my life and love me, but just being on the social media platform listening to her ministering me back to life is blessing my whole life. When I wrote my first book, I felt that I was literally killing myself, because I was so depressed. I took the hurt and disappointments of my childhood and not being loved into my adulthood. But recently connecting with Real Talk Kim, I've learned to love me and accept that life is just what it is, *life*. And in order to get to the next level, I must go through certain things to come out on fire. It took forty-three years and Real Talk Kim [for me] to understand my worth. I love Real Talk Kim so much. I wake up and go to sleep with her podcast and I'm like a kid in a candy store when it comes to *Live at Nine* and Inner Circle. I'm getting through this, and I am a winner!

–N

we have turned, every one, to his own way; and the LORD has laid on Him the iniquity of us all.

—ISAIAH 53:5–6

Understand God's Plan

If you can see the grand scheme of your life, you will see that Jesus didn't go to the cross because the Jewish people wanted Him dead. He could have called ten thousand angels to deliver Him from Calvary. Instead, He remained on that cross and took your sins so you could have eternal life. "He personally carried our sins in his body on the cross so that we can be dead to sin and live for what is right. By his wounds you are healed" (1 Pet. 2:24, NLT).

Testimony

I have been following Kim for three years. She has really opened my eyes to the person I was. Then I listened, I did–and now I am changed! With her being so real and down to earth, it really helps you listen! I have been set free from anxiety, people-pleasing, and [I have] put God first place in my life! Her ministry/church has changed and blessed my whole life! Thank you, Real Talk Kim!

–M

You cannot be good enough, work hard enough, or be famous enough to earn your salvation. The scripture from 1 Peter tells us that Jesus took into His own body all the sins that we would ever commit. He did it so we could die to our sins, be free of sin, and be healed. That life-sustaining promise helps me to forgive myself for everything that I allowed to happen in my life, and it helps me to forgive everyone who ever wronged me. Then I can ask the Lord for forgiveness and know that He has promised me everlasting life.

You see, before we were even born, God had a plan!

Today's Declaration

Lord, I decree and declare that my crooked paths are straightened and the mountains of doubt in my life are melting like wax. Thank You for restoration, restitution, and regeneration. I am a new creation in Christ Jesus, and my past will never resurface.

CHAPTER 7

I'm Not Who You Say I Am

LIVING OUT THE labels that family and friends give you can keep you from walking in your God-given destiny. You must decide that you will look to God, not people, for affirmation. Let Him define you by His labels, which bless and do not curse you. I can tell you that I spent too many years comparing myself with others and thinking that I could never measure up. That less-than mentality drove me to make decisions that were detrimental not only to me but also to the generations after me.

Isn't it amazing that God made us one of a kind, yet we beat up ourselves trying to be like everybody else? In essence, we try to become God by deciding when we're on our game and when we're worthless. Even when no one is judging us, we judge ourselves. We are our harshest critics, and we convince ourselves that everyone sees us as negatively as we do.

My dad always told me that I was just like his mom, Sudie Mae, who died when I was very small. Because she wasn't there as I grew up, she became (in my mind) the mystery lady known as Grandma. I assumed that I looked just like her, and I began searching for pictures that would prove it. When my dad showed me one, I was shocked. Grandma was five feet ten inches tall and weighed at least 250 pounds. She was an older woman at the time, with gray hair fixed in a bun on top of her head. I obviously inherited her height, but that was where the resemblance fell apart. We didn't even share similar hair or eye color.

Grandma's picture haunted me, not because she wasn't pretty or stylish, but because she weighed much more than I did. Because my mom is so petite, I always worried about weight, even as a child. Now my dad was showing me a picture of his mom, who didn't care a lick that she was heavy. And he was telling me that I reminded him of her!

I'm sure that if I had grown up knowing Grandma personally, I would have looked past her height, weight, eye color, and bun to see the sweet lady whom my dad loved very much. And once I got over her weight in the photo, I realized that what my dad saw in me was her height, especially since my mom is only five feet two inches tall. (Dad is above average height himself, at five foot eleven.) At birth, I was a little five-pound bundle who came out butt first with one leg wrapped around my head.

My dad always said my mom was a wonder woman because she gave birth to me without an epidural, which most women would request when delivering a breech baby. Mom became my wonder woman, too, because I believed she could take care of anything. She always made my brother and me feel like we were the most special people in the whole world. In fact, she poured out so much love that, in my teenage years, I resented her always being there and I was eager to break out. Whether she was volunteering as the school nurse or band parent, my mom did whatever it took to be present in our lives.

It's amazing that, as awesome as my mom was, I found fault. Apparently, my friends saw her more clearly, because as I was pulling away, they were drawn to her and loved coming to see her. She was Mom to all of them, and I resented that they loved her so much. In fact, all the girls at my parents' church wanted to stay at our house. I did not understand what they loved about our family, but something drew them in. I may have been the only one who did not recognize how special our family was.

That is what happens when you are driven by your emotions. You can spend time and energy trying to be like some people and not like others. You cannot see the world as it is, and the world never sees the real you. I didn't know who I wanted to be, but I knew I didn't like the *me* that God created. I was never happy with myself. I wanted to be like other people, and I wanted my family to look like their families. I lived behind a façade that hid my identity. Even I didn't begin to know who I was until I was thirty-six years of age.

In my opinion, all families are irregular and none are perfect. However, certain families deal differently than others when life throws them curves. These families do not allow circumstances to determine their altitude. Whether they suffer financial lack or sickness, they seem to know how to make life work for them.

Looking back, I can see that my family was one of them. Someone even told me recently that she loves our family because we never know when to quit. We just keep expecting God to do a greater work tomorrow. Oh, to go back in time and be thankful for who I was and what God had given me!

Contentment

It's clear to me now that I had never learned to be content in my earlier life. That came much later, but thank God, it came! The apostle Paul had a solid grasp on being content. I think it was because he understood the power of the Holy Spirit. It was through the Spirit that Paul learned to be content and could say, "Not that I speak in regard to need, for I have learned in whatever state I am, to be content" (Phil. 4:11).

Finding contentment has a lot to do with accepting who you are and who God created you to be. Are you content? Do you have a clear sense of who you are? If not, simply ask yourself right now, "Who am I?" If you are going to glean anything from this book, you will have to honestly answer that question or at least admit that you're not quite sure what the answer is.

I know what that's like. I remember walking into my dad's office one day when his pastor friend was visiting. The man immediately asked me, "How did you get to be an Amazon?"

Obviously, he wasn't referring to the online marketplace but to very tall women in Greek mythology. To me, the statement became a point of comparison for almost everything I did from that day forward. My imagination took over, and I saw myself as bigger than everyone else. I began comparing myself to everyone in my family and wondering, "Why was I born so tall? Why, God, did You make me so different? Why am I such a klutz? What is wrong with this picture?"

While my petite mom complains that she is too short, I have asked a thousand times why I was not born shorter. At the age of twelve, I skipped right over my mom's shoe size, going straight from a size five to a seven. As a result, I was never able to wear my mom's shoes. Not only was I super tall, but my feet also seemed to grow in direct proportion to the rest of my body!

Not all my complaints were physical. I was already dealing with learning disabilities and wondering how it was possible for my brother and me to perform so differently at school. He excelled in his studies, but I couldn't solve simple math problems. "Surely," I thought, "I've done so much wrong that God is punishing me."

Finding contentment has a lot to do with accepting who you are and who God created you to be.

Discontentment is not a good place to be. I wondered how I could trust a God who made me so broken that I could not be or do anything right. Are you getting this picture? I could not figure out who Kimberly was created to be, other than something less than everybody else. Being a loser seemed to be my only fate.

Now, by the grace of God, I know that He never created me or anybody else to be a loser. Not even one of us is less than in His eyes.

Unlikely Does Not Mean Unwanted

Do you feel as though you are always moving in a downward direction? Do you feel unable to stop the constant judging, comparing, and inward negative voices that say you cannot accomplish anything? Do you question why anyone should believe in you when you don't believe in yourself?

I have been there. To finally begin my journey of healing, I had to lose all that God had given me and have a personal awakening. I mentioned this earlier, but let me explain another aspect of what I mean. During one of our moves, my husband and I moved to Orlando and assumed that we would be on staff at a local church. Our assumptions did not come to fruition, so we arrived in a new city with no income in sight. But somehow, God opened a door for me to begin a new journey.

A friend who had a great eye for design and I were given the opportunity to do a church makeover. It gave me a reason to get up the next day. We changed the colors of the walls, made floral arrangements, and bought accessories that transformed the look of the church. To my surprise, everyone loved the finished product.

That was the beginning of a new business! We were paid for our efforts, and people affirmed our work. I realized that I was good at managing people and lining up more business opportunities. Soon, we were a full-fledged company. I had not gone out looking for this type of business and had no idea that I was gifted to make other people's worlds prettier. Even today, I'm definitely not the norm. I am not the type who shops at regular department stores. I am very colorful and always choose clothes that most people would not consider wearing. I know I don't look like a runway model in my boots and layered outfits, and I'm all right with that. It took me decades to let other people see who God made me to be. I no longer try to fit in with everybody else. I've learned that

I'm not supposed to be like them (which is why conforming never worked for me).

Don't you know that when Persia's King Xerxes chose Esther, a young Hebrew woman, to be his queen, she could not yet see herself standing at his side? She was an orphan raised by her cousin Mordecai. She had no dowry to offer a king. She wasn't raised by royalty and did not know how to act like a queen. In fact, she was a despised Jew among Gentiles.

In my opinion, Esther would never have become Xerxes' queen had Mordecai not believed that she was ready for the position. If it had been up to Esther, she would not have seen herself as being up to the task. However, God had a plan for her, as He does for each of us. Once Esther got on board, it was her responsibility to prepare herself for that plan, which she did. With the help of Hegai, the eunuch in charge of the harem of candidates for queen, Esther became everything the king desired in his bride.

Esther's beauty quickly won her favor and special attention from Hegai. Whatever he instructed Esther to do, she did. When she finally went before the king, he was immediately taken with her. He found Esther to be the most attractive candidate, and he placed the royal crown on her head.

God will send the right people to help set your promotion in motion.

This young Jewish woman had no idea that God would use her to save the Jews from annihilation. Yet the Bible says that God chose her for the role. Mordecai sensed it too and asked her, "Who knows if perhaps you were made queen for just such a time as this?" (Est. 4:14, NLT).

Remember that God is "no respecter of persons" (Acts 10:34, KJV). If He chose an unknown orphan girl and made her queen, He has great plans for you too. God will send the right people to help set your promotion in motion.

What You Believe Matters

When all you see is the loser in you, when all you hear in your head are judgments against you, you are not capable of receiving from the people God sends to encourage you through your journey. You might even believe that you have no encouragers because all you can remember are the people who put you down.

Could it be that you are not seeing what you are not open to seeing? Maybe you haven't allowed yourself to embrace opportunities for growth and have unknowingly dismissed the very people God sent to assist you on your journey.

Believe me, I'm not pointing the finger—except maybe at myself. This is *exactly* what I did for years. So, I know what it's like to reject people for the wrong reasons. I rejected the people God sent to help me because I saw them only through my self-inflicted pain. I could not believe in myself. Therefore, I could not believe that anyone would want to help me.

I now know a little more about what was going on. I know what John 10:10 says about our enemy, Satan, wanting to steal, kill, and destroy our future. He attacks anyone God promotes. (If you are under attack, promotion is probably coming.) But God warns us to be watchful of the enemy's schemes. First Peter 5:8 says, "Stay alert! Watch out for your great enemy, the devil. He prowls around like a roaring lion, looking for someone to devour" (NLT). Satan continually harasses us because he wants to destroy our lives and keep us from the joy of relationship with our Lord Jesus.

Can you imagine the attacks Esther must have faced? She suffered great loss in her life and probably never imagined herself sitting on a throne. Had she not begun to believe that she was destined and assigned by God, she would not have believed Mordecai's insight into her destiny. She had no idea that she was being placed in the Persian kingdom to intercede for the Jewish people. God gave her enormous favor with King Xerxes, who would otherwise have accepted the advice of his chief minister, Haman. Haman was intent on destroying the Jews, and he almost succeeded in doing so. But God had a plan, as He always does, and He worked His plan through Esther.

It's easy to judge the unlikely people God sends your way and doubt the benefits of their presence in your life. Esther was a great asset to Xerxes and to her people, but she was not born into royalty. In and of herself, she was not prepared to do what Mordecai believed she could do. Yet, with faith and a willingness to follow instruction, she became well equipped for her assignment.

You might feel totally unready to take back the ground Satan has stolen from you, but remember this: you have already survived things you thought for sure would take you out. And you will survive whatever you are facing now. Neither the opinions of others nor the lies the devil whispers in your ear will determine your destination unless you let them. What you believe matters, and only what God says really counts.

So, do what I did: tell yourself (hundreds of times if necessary), "I'm not who they say I am. I will not allow those who judge me to destroy me with their words. I can do all things through Christ who strengthens me."

It's Always Growing Season

God has declared the new—a new day, a new relationship, a new business, a new marriage. It's your responsibility to step into it. Don't allow a sense of being alone or lonely to determine your direction. Don't allow yourself to become codependent with others because you don't know how to be alone with yourself.

Do you have any idea how wonderful a creation you are? God did that! When friends and family overlook you, you can easily take it personally, feel sorry for yourself, and assume that no one cares. But what if God is separating you from certain people so He can change your direction? What if this "silent season" is a growing season? Those are the times when you learn who God created you to be. Honestly, you cannot even recognize your resilience until you have been rejected. You cannot know your strength until you have been through pain. You are stronger and more resilient than you realize.

Esther could not have known the strength that was within her until Mordecai prompted her to approach the king about Haman's plan to annihilate the Jews. In that day, a queen could not enter the king's presence uninvited. If she did, she risked death. Esther knew this. She approached the king with trepidation but also a willingness to die for the sake of obeying God. Because she acted in spite of the danger, she is remembered to this day for saving God's people.

Do you wonder who you were created to be? Have you sought the Lord about His intentions for your future? Do you realize yet that you can't walk your path alone? You need someone to assist you with your destiny. (Everyone does.) The enemy isn't trying to kill you; he's trying to stop the deliverer within you. He's not after who you are. He's after who you are going to become. It took me years to learn this, but you can learn it by the time you turn this page.

Today, I can look in the face of the opposition the enemy brings and laugh. Why? Because I have been through the fire and I came out in one piece. I may have slowed down for six years to get my life on track, but during that time, I saw my destiny up close. I realized that the call on my life was greater than any pain I ever endured.

I remember a certain day when I was four years old and playing with my dolls. My mother overheard me telling my dolls that I wanted to preach but that I thought I would have to sing instead, because my daddy did not believe in women preachers. At the time, we were in a religious organization that believed women could teach children but not lead men in a church.

Isn't it ironic that I now travel around the world preaching to men and women in churches—even megachurches? Can you see why Satan wanted to take me out? He wanted to steal the call to the nations that God had placed within my heart. He wanted to wear me out doing life the way I had arranged it so I would never have the energy to chase after God.

The enemy will do anything necessary to create havoc enough to blind you to the person God created you to be. He's betting that you will lose faith in your purpose, which is the reason for your life. Could it be that the enemy sees more greatness in you than you see in yourself?

God Is Ready to Go When You Let Go

God is ready to work with you when you are ready to walk with Him. It has nothing to do with what people say about you. It really is about your choices. No one could have written the plan for my life as it is today. Even my parents who loved me unreservedly could not have foreseen my life as it is now.

One of the greatest lessons for me has been understanding how to accept and love the person God created me to be. I had to learn contentment in that. For a time, I clung to certain people, not realizing that they were limiting my elevation in the Spirit. I had become codependent, needing their affirmations. I did not know how to allow God to be my Lord in all things. But when I gave up and said "It's over," I stepped out of the less-than mentality and into a blessing mentality. I am still amazed at how easy it was! I moved on from the very people I thought I couldn't live without. I no longer needed their affirmations to make my decisions. I realized that I could think

Testimony

Pastor Kim appeared in my life through social media, right when I needed her. Like her, I was never a fan of organized religion but was raised in the Baptist church. I was going through an incredibly tough time in my life. I had a new baby and was having a terrible time with my husband's family. It was through Kim and her straight talking (which being an Australian was just my speed) that I examined my life [and] what I wanted for my future, and worked through the conflicts in my life and how I was going to have to move forward without an apology. Not only did she relight my spark for my life, but [she] also made me realize I was never alone, and God had been speaking to me and blessing my life this whole time. I love her so hard for that. A true blessing from God!

–A

for myself. The cobwebs were clearing out of my mind, and God's direction was becoming clearer.

God is asking you to do some hard things right now because breakthrough is coming and you need to be ready. You are not who people say you are. You are one of a kind. Don't allow fear to determine your destination. You will not end up alone. When you allow God to be Lord of your life, you and He are a majority.

I am still flabbergasted at how God replaced my bosom buddies, drinking buddies, and partying buddies with thousands of loyal partners who keep me covered in prayer day and night. One of my greatest revelations has been realizing that some people don't want you to live your best life. The secret to your success is to not become one of them. It's so much easier to do and understand than you might realize. A certain quote has summed it up for me: "Weak people seek revenge, strong people forgive, and intelligent people ignore."[1]

When you decide to walk in forgiveness, it won't matter what people say. When you start living your life to its fullest, you won't have time to worry about the people who are trying to steal your future. Here's another gem to keep in mind: "If you quit now, you'll end up right back where you began. And when you first began, you were desperate to be where you are right now. Keep going!"[2]

Testimony

I've suffered for sixteen years from bipolar, depression, anxiety, and suicidal tendencies, trying anything and everything I could to hide from them. Alcohol, drugs, and toxic relationships [too]. In December of 2013, after leaving my kids' father, I tried to commit suicide, and God said, "Not today." In February of 2014, the Lord took my mother and my best friend home to be with Him, and I crumbled. Alcohol, drugs, and bad decisions were just my lifestyle. I made a lot of decisions while intoxicated that I never would have [made] sober. I had promised my mom that I would never try to hurt myself again, and up until I lost my $60,000+ a year job in July of this year, I never had. After I lost my job, I sank and hit rock bottom and sat in my bathroom one night contemplating it. Two days later, I walked into the church my mom went to for service, and a couple days after that I found a Real Talk Kim sermon. Since then I've been immersed in it. Sermons, Bible reading, praises, Real Talk Kim, and the Inner Circle. I've been intentional as much as I can be, in all aspects. I slowly began feeling myself change. I no longer wish to not wake up; I thank God for waking me. I'm starting to praise my way out of everything because I am a child of God and He loves me, and I am worthy of love. Kim has taught me so much already in just the six weeks I've been following her. And there's still so much to do. I'm rewiring my head and changing my character. And for the first time in sixteen years, I can say I have more good days than I do bad. Kim, being so real, gave me someone to connect with and feel like someone else understands. I worry less and pray more. I find myself drawn to God's Word and love more than I ever have. Kim's a real person, with a real past, and that is just something to which I can relate.

–A

Today's Declaration

Lord, I decree and declare that all things are made new in my life. It's a new chapter, and I refuse to be ruled by my past any longer. I choose to receive Your promises and Your unmerited grace. I invite Your love to overflow in me, and I am contagious with Your love and power. Thank You for Your mercy and grace.

CHAPTER 8

Avoiding the Comparison Trap

WITH SO MANY social media platforms at our fingertips, it's easy to be consumed with scrolling through other people's highlight reels. If we are not careful, we end up wishing we had their lives instead of our own. We get trapped in forgetting how great life really is and how fearfully and wonderfully made we really are.

During my twenties, a Rusk hair representative stopped me in the mall and asked me to participate in a hair show. I was so amazed that they would choose me. I mean, I was the one who never looked good, never did anything well, and certainly would add no value to a modeling show. Yet, even though I imagined myself stumbling on the runway or falling over my own feet, I agreed to participate.

Of the one hundred models chosen, I was the final one featured. They saved me for last because my hair needed so much help. They said it was too coarse and my brunette color was outdated. By the time they finished describing my hair, I was ready for them to do anything they could to fix it.

I let them cut off all my gorgeous long hair and color it red, even though I didn't like the color at that time.

Do you see what happened? Until I saw my "before" pictures, I did not realize that my long, dark hair was pretty. Now I sported a short, red look and didn't even recognize the person in the mirror. I had acted impulsively because I allowed my emotions to take over. Once they did, they mapped out my direction, attitude, and altitude. I let the opinions of strangers turn me into someone I didn't even know.

I'm sure I'm not the only one who's made an emotional decision. I'm guessing you have made some too. So, I'm OK with being a prime example of how such failures happen and how we can recover from them.

Unexpected Reminder

When I discovered social media, I was still living with my parents after a marriage failure. Every evening after work, I would come home, eat, and head straight for the solitude of my room. It was during this time that I found Myspace, which opened a whole new realm of comparing myself with others.

The greatest insight I remember gaining in that time started with a fact list that had gone viral. It was called "25 Random Things About Me." Maybe you remember it. People would list their favorite things and other facts about themselves. I remember telling myself, "You don't have any favorites. You have no idea who you really are because you have lived to please others your entire life."

Immediately, I began sobbing. My life was a wreck. I really didn't know myself, and I didn't know how to fix that. In the midst of my reeling, my younger son came to my room. He was only thirteen at the time, so other than being supportive, how could he help? Yet, two weeks later, on Mother's Day morning, that boy gave me the most precious gift I would ever receive. It was a poem that he composed and framed, just for me. It changed my life.

Get your tissues as you read it!

> You are beautiful, you are kind
> You love me when I am annoying
> You sing like an angel
> You buy me things
> You work hard for my needs, you provide for me
> You make the world stop when you laugh
> You give me hugs that make me love you
> more and more each day
> You don't complain when you are mad
> You make people happy with your smile
> You care for me, you cry with me when I am sad
> You love those who hate, you make the world different
> You are a superwoman
> You somehow become friends with your enemies
> You laugh at bad memories
> You survived hell in high heels
> You are triumphant
> You yell at me with a grin
> You make people feel beautiful
> You make me feel very appreciative
> You give me things I don't deserve
> You make me laugh when you yell at me
> You make other moms jealous
> You don't care what other people think about you
> You snuggle with me
> You scream my name at basketball games
> You smile like the sun, you are unlike any other
> You bought me Christmas gifts when you didn't have to

You always smell good
You don't take crap from anyone
You laugh at mistakes
You forgive me when I make mistakes
You give me grace
You say "sorry" when you make mistakes
You love God
You laugh at my jokes even when they're not funny
You give me advice; you tell me that everything is okay
My favorite thing that I love about you is that...
You are you

—LYNCOLN DOGGETT

How in the world could you read a poem like that from a boy who means the world to you and not decide to change? Lyncoln wrote those words at one of the lowest points in my life. It was a beautiful demonstration of God's love for me. Amazingly, my son knew me better than I knew myself. I'm still awestruck by how God used him to put me on my knees, where I would finally seek Him and learn about the woman He had created me to be.

God used what I saw as my time of greatest failure to catapult me into the ministry of healing. One of the lines in Lyncoln's poem declared that I "survived hell in high heels." I had no idea that I was surviving at all. As far as I could tell, I was washed up and left for dead. But my son saw strength in me when I didn't see it in myself. Because of his poem, my ministry was initially called Conquering Hell in High Heels.

Humble Beginnings, Strong Finish

Have you ever thought about the boy David who became the greatest king in biblical history? He didn't start out that way.

He wrote many psalms, including Psalm 69, which covers a twenty-eight-year period of his life from his childhood to his coronation. In it, he shares the heartache of being a lonely shepherd boy left to care for his father's flock, a sibling despised by his brothers, a person without the comfort of friends, and a man surrounded by enemies.[1] He wrote, "Those who hate me without reason outnumber the hairs of my head; many are my enemies without cause, those who seek to destroy me" (Ps. 69:4, NIV). He talked about being "a stranger to [his] brothers" (v. 8), a family member who felt no right of belonging in his family.

In Psalm 69, "David passionately gives voice to the heaviest burdens of his soul." Talk about a dysfunctional family! David's brothers believed their baby brother would never measure up to their family's standards. Their father, Jesse, was a venerated head of the Sanhedrin, so the standards were high. Through no fault of his own, David grew up under a cloud of criticism and judgmentalism.[2]

It is peculiar that the son of "one of the most distinguished leaders of his generation" would be so forsaken. If you or I were born into a king's family, we would be honored just for being royalty. But David never enjoyed that privilege. His birth drew "utter derision and contempt." David described the environment of his upbringing, saying, "I was a stranger to my brothers, a foreigner to my mother's sons."[3]

Scholars have speculated as to why David was so viciously rejected, but that's a story for another day. The point here is how God turned his life around. Who would believe that this young man could become king of Israel? Certainly not his brothers! Imagine how they felt when Samuel the prophet came looking for a king and rejected each of them because God said, "This is not the one." (See 1 Samuel 16:6–10). God sent Samuel to Jesse's house with the express purpose of anointing one of Jesse's sons, but Samuel was looking for God's *chosen* king.

Jesse never even thought to include his son David in the selection process. Being the family outcast was nothing new for David. He wasn't even "permitted to eat with the rest of the family, but was assigned to a separate table in the corner."[4] Certainly, Jesse and his seven oldest sons never imagined young David becoming the king of Israel. They were sure that God would choose one of Jesse's gifted and favored offspring.

They did not see what God saw. They did not know what God knew. Even Samuel did not know who the king would be. Yet God had already chosen David. Now He would make His choice known to Samuel and David's family. When Samuel saw Jesse's eldest son, Eliab, Samuel thought he looked like a perfect choice. But God said no. He told Samuel to "look not at the outside but at the inside."[5]

Samuel wisely decided to wait on God's selection. After considering seven sons, with no success, Samuel asked, "Is there another son?" (See 1 Samuel 16:11.) When Jesse said that his youngest was out with the sheep, Samuel asked that the young man be brought to him.

You know the rest of the story. David was anointed king of Israel. Rejection had plagued his life, but God was David's recompense!

How many times have you felt that your family or peers would never accept you? How long have you suffered while awaiting justice? How long have you felt that no one understood your pain, suffering, and loneliness? If David were here today, I'm sure he could tell you that the end result described in Jeremiah 29:11 is worth the wait.

David became the most honored king in the history of Israel. What was said of the Messiah in Psalm 118:22 was also fulfilled in David's life, in the presence of people who once discounted him: "The stone which the builders rejected has become the chief cornerstone."[6]

Although David's writings plainly express his suffering, they also reveal "his faith and conviction."[7] Had it been up to his brothers, David would always have been a poor, lonely shepherd. But God! He still had a plan for David, and He has one for you.

Refuse to allow people who don't know you to define you.

You will hear me say this time and again, whether I am preaching or mentoring: "It's not over until God says it's over." So, allow David to be your example. Refuse to allow people who don't know you to define you.

One good thing about going through hell is that you come out on fire! David was a game changer, a nation shaker. However, those closest to him could not see his greatness. His brothers were not with him on the mountainside when he sought the Lord and fought off the mountain lion. They had no clue that David could stand up to danger and come out a winner. All they had were their preconceived ideas. There was no way, in their minds, that the brother they saw as a loser could be anointed king.

Yet he was. Thank God that David did not spend his days

worrying about measuring up to his older siblings. He just cared for the sheep and trusted his God. I wonder what he thought when he arrived at the anointing service and saw all his brothers staring at him. I personally think he was ready for the anointing, because every day on the hillside with the flock, he had been setting the atmosphere for the supernatural. He played his harp, sang songs unto the God of Israel, and walked out his responsibilities as a shepherd. It didn't look like preparation for the throne, but it was.

It doesn't matter how your situation looks or how dysfunctional your family is. Maybe no one has ever believed in you. Maybe you were the family outcast. But it doesn't matter because God has the last word.

Right this second, you are reading this book, which I believe was ordained by God. That makes you different from a lot of people around you. Deep down, you sense that you are a David for your generation. A game changer. A nation shaker. A giant destroyer. You just have to *believe* that God made you unique for a purpose.

Would you like to change something about yourself? Would you like to be more confident or charismatic? Do you wish you were more popular and outgoing but less anxious? Most everyone is seeking some kind of change in his or her life. I don't know many people who are completely satisfied with who they are or even who God made them to be. The question is whether you will allow peripheral issues to determine your altitude. Instead, let the realization that you are distinct *for a reason* help you to live contented while God assists you in becoming the person He has in mind.

Resurrection Power

Have you ever wondered why you can't seem to change? People ask me this question in nearly every seminar and conference in which I speak. They tell me that they want to change but don't have the willpower to carry it out. They go to conferences, revival meetings, and seminars seeking the cure for their issues. They are trying to find the perfect diet, the right health regimen, the best routine for making the drastic changes they desire. Then the changes they struggle to achieve last for a day or a week or, sometimes, only a few hours.

One good thing about going through hell is that you come out on fire!

I understand. I have been on that roller coaster dozens of times. I am not like my mother, who has spent her whole life weighing the same 105 pounds soaking wet. I'm not sure I ever hit that mark on my way up to my present weight (which I will not be discussing). I can tell you that I don't spend my days comparing myself to my mom or even my sister-in-love, who is one of the greatest cooks I know. I'm aware of my limitations; but I also know my strengths. I might not be as petite as my mom, and I might not know how to boil water. But I sure can preach until the sky looks level, and I will pray for hundreds to receive their deliverance.

Are you getting this? I am finally happy with the *me* God made. What about you? You know you want change, and you want it now. You want to get unstuck and free from comparisons. So, ask yourself the questions that Pastor Rick Warren poses: "Where do we get the power to change? How do we get our lives out of neutral?"[8]

Let me suggest a simple answer: Jesus Christ offers us freedom from our self-doubt and negative decisions. He offers us the resurrection power that is available because He went to the cross, was buried, went to hell, and now holds the keys to death and hell. (See Revelation 1:18.) Plus, He set the captives free! This is why we can be called righteous. Jesus became sin for us and made it possible for us to live again. The apostle Paul explains it this way:

> I have been crucified with Christ; it is no longer I who live, but Christ lives in me; and the life which I now live in the flesh I live by faith in the Son of God, who loved me and gave Himself for me.
>
> —GALATIANS 2:20

We know that Paul was not literally nailed to the cross with Jesus. Yet he knew that Jesus had fulfilled His promise and taken our sins (every sin we would commit for a lifetime) so that we could be set free when we were ready to accept what He did for us.

We cannot overstate the significance of what Jesus did. Warren says that "the word *power* occurs fifty-seven times in the New Testament. It is used to describe the...resurrection of Jesus Christ from the dead." The mortal part of His being died, and He came back to life so we could have eternal life with Him. That same "resurrection power is available to change your life!"[9]

The most important decision you will ever make is to know Jesus Christ and experience the power of His resurrection. The apostle Paul made that decision and said this:

> I want to know Christ and experience the mighty power that raised him from the dead. I want to suffer with him, sharing in his death, so that one way or another I will experience the resurrection from the dead!
>
> —PHILIPPIANS 3:10–11, NLT

Paul knew he would suffer at the hands of hypocritical Jews, because he had been a major player in their ranks. In fact, he was once at the forefront of punishing Christians for believing in the Christ he now preached. Paul was completely transformed by a visitation from Christ and became so sold out that he was ready to lay down his life for the gospel.

Paul experienced resurrection power firsthand. He knew that if he could open our understanding to the greatness of that power, we would choose to believe that anything is possible for us. Therefore, he wrote passages like this one:

> I also pray that you will understand the incredible greatness of God's power for us who believe him. This is the same mighty power that raised Christ from the dead and seated him in the place of honor at God's right hand in the heavenly realms.
>
> —EPHESIANS 1:19–20, NLT

Do you believe what Paul said? Then you do not have to live a life of comparison with those around you. You are one of a kind, and no one can measure up to you. Look at what Warren says about the power just mentioned in Ephesians:

> Paul uses the Greek word for power, *dunamis,* which is the root of our word *dynamite.* So Paul is saying, "God wants to give you dynamite power that can

> change your life." Yes, the same power that raised Jesus Christ from the dead...is available to us right now to transform the weaknesses in our lives into strengths.[10]

Everything you just read is true if you have accepted Jesus Christ as your Lord and Savior. One of my greatest joys is knowing that this power has canceled my past and given me the brightest future. That is so freeing!

When you feel like you have failed everyone and you cannot figure out your tomorrow, it's time to quit trying to do it yourself. Allow God's power to change you from the inside out. You do not have to live in other people's shadows, comparing their accomplishments with yours. You do not have to live in regret for all the things you have done. In an instant, God can change you from within.

Even God tells us that we don't have to be weighed down

Testimony

Real Talk Kim has changed my way of thinking. I have been following her since 2014 when she was on the side of the road in her car making videos. I was so broken. I was at rock bottom, but I found Jesus was the Rock at the bottom. I was so hurt, my world was dark at that very moment when I found her! It was just me and my two girls at the time. I had just gotten out of a thirteen-year relationship. My first boyfriend ever (my girls' dad) and I went through hell and came out on *fiyah*!!! I even talk like RTK now (lol)! I wrote a letter to God, prayed over it every night, did my part, and let God be God. I prayed for a king, that's even my last name now (go God, go), and He blessed me with two—my now husband and a son. We were living in a two-bedroom apartment, but now we own our home, paid off some debt, because I couldn't buy cheese with my credit either. I lost both my parents within ten months apart but I tell you, with God, RTK, and my husband, I've pushed through! #boom #wonthedoit. I love ...you RTK! Mmuuuaahhh.

—T

by guilt and shame. When we choose to give up, "he cancels our past,"[11] just as Scripture says: "God…forgave us all our sins, having canceled the charge of our legal indebtedness, which stood against us and condemned us; he has taken it away, nailing it to the cross" (Col. 2:13–14, NIV).

How can I assure you that if you ask God's forgiveness, He will forgive every wrong you have ever done? I understand the hesitation. It almost seems too easy to be true. But on the cross, Jesus made an earth-shattering statement: "It is finished." In the Greek, it means "paid in full, canceled." Therefore, you never have to walk in condemnation for the things you've done or allowed. "Jesus was crucified on the cross so that we could stop crucifying ourselves."[12]

Jesus took all your pain and humiliation that day on Calvary. "He was hung up for our hang-ups."[13] He made you more than a conqueror. Never again do you have to allow your past choices to rule and reign over you. It is *over*. However, you must decide that it's over. It is up to you!

Testimony

I've been following Real Talk Kim for years now. Let me tell you this, she is as real in person as she is online. What you see is what you get. She is so warm and loving. Like she really loves people for real. I got the opportunity to meet her at my church in Virginia. As I stood in line to talk to her, I watched her greet each and every one of the ladies with a genuine embrace and smile. And that line was long. By the time I made it up to see her, I thought for sure she would be exhausted, but she greeted me like we were long lost friends. Support everything she does, y'all. She's the real deal.

–T

Today's Declaration

I decree and declare that I will not be impatient. I will wait on the Lord to renew my strength. Lord, give me the strength not to submit to the world's ways or even the way my family has done things. Let me be a generational curse breaker. I know You have assigned every step of my life. Thank You for reviving every godly dream and hope that has been shattered. Thank You for making even the impossible achievable for me. Thank You for helping me to become alert and watchful as a child of God. In Jesus' name, amen.

Part III: The Real Me

CHAPTER 9

Designed by the Master

Before God formed us, He knew that we would face horrific seasons of mistakes and would end up feeling less than. Then we act as though life has written us off and put us on the clearance rack. But we can choose to get out of that pity party and put ourselves back on the couture rack where we belong. Then our messes will become our message, and our scars will turn to stars. Remember: God has qualified us. So, no matter what society tells us, *it ain't over.*

Several years ago, before I found the *me* whom God created, I lived in everyone else's shadow. My then husband and I were living a life of less than while watching others live in more than enough. Because of our situation, people sometimes blessed us with the nice suits or branded shoes they no longer needed. I still own a St. John suit someone gifted to me during those lean times. I keep it as a reminder of the life from which God delivered me.

Back when I wore that suit, people saw me and thought I was fitting in. At least, that was my impression. In that suit I felt like a totally different woman—one who had it all together and was as affluent as everyone else in the room. But deep down I knew I was still less than. I needed more than the temporary fix of looking good on the outside. I needed to know within my being that my life would change.

It would take more than a St. John suit to do that. For some reason, I didn't understand that even without affluence I was specially designed by God for a purpose only I could fill. Don't you know that if I'd had even a clue of what my life would be today, I would have changed years sooner? But that's the way life rolls.

You see, the Book of Hebrews tells us that "faith is the substance of things hoped for, the evidence of things not seen" (11:1). Even after being raised in a preacher's home, I did not have that kind of faith. I did not understand about having a true relationship with Jesus Christ. I suppose I thought that life was all about works and that nothing would happen unless I instigated it. Of course, I know now that life is much bigger than that.

Even when I was making a great income, I did not realize that Jesus Christ was in charge of my life—or that He should be. Whether I suffered from lack or had plenty of money, I did not know how to face tomorrow. When the big money was coming in, I hoarded it in my little fireproof safe so it would be at my disposal whenever I needed it. My mom talks about when I visited her with my little friend, my safe, by my side. I wouldn't let it out of my sight. Whom could I trust? No one had made that money but me, so why should I trust anyone to take care of it like I would? Once I lost everything, I realized that my empty safe meant nothing to me.

My "savior" was the money that used to be in the safe. Now, that my "savior" had checked out, what would I do?

My answer might (or might not) surprise you: I called on God first and my parents second. I finally realized that I had a team rooting for my victory. That was awesome, but now I had to learn about the real me. It was clear that I could not buy happiness. Happiness is fleeting anyway. It's like when you get a new outfit and think you won't need any more new clothes for a while. But once you wear your new garb, the happy goes away. So, you buy the next thing you think will make you happy again.

When you start to discover who you are, you don't want that fleeting feeling anymore. It definitely lost its luster for me. I wanted the joy you get when you receive Jesus Christ in your life and become acquainted with the person you were long before you started making crazy choices. That's when you can look back and realize who you aren't. That's what happened to me. I realized that the St. John suit never was my style. It took some time for me to realize my value, but I finally got it. And guess what? I found I'm more of a Betsey Johnson girl.

Even after going through my divorce and losing my company and home, I was moving into a new season and receiving invitations to preach. It was amazing! Yet I still battled the old less-than mentality. When I rehearse those days now, I realize that other people were not my problem. It was all about me. I had never figured out how God could love me in spite of what I had done. I didn't understand how He could accept me as I was or bless me while asking only for my love. So, He began blessing me on purpose, even when I wasn't asking. Ministry invitations kept me so busy that I hired an assistant to help with my scheduling. All this and I was still coming to grips with the real me.

Coming Off the Clearance Rack

One day, my assistant and I were posting pictures on Instagram. Like most people, I didn't like the way I looked, so I downloaded an app that would change my whole appearance. I stretched my body to make it look slenderer, and I erased my wrinkles so I would look younger. I was really pleased with the finished product, so I uploaded it. My son messaged me immediately and told me to take a closer look at the photo. Not only had the app stretched my body, but it had also made my feet look at least four sizes longer. I quickly deleted that picture and decided that I would be whoever God created me to be. Another lesson learned!

It took time for me to come off the clearance rack. There is a woman in the Bible who could testify to that process. I'm sure she was talked about and written off by everyone because of the life she led. (I can relate to her life, because some people talked about me and my unwise choices back in the day.) She was known as a sinner. We don't know for sure why, but it really doesn't matter. At one time or another, all of us have been judged harshly, sometimes without reason. The sin we all commit is one of the givens of our mortality. One of the mysteries of life is that some are judged more harshly than others.

This woman's story is one of the greatest examples of forgiveness and redemption I've ever heard. She is the woman who washed Jesus' feet when He was invited to dinner at a Pharisee's house. The place was filled with men who were eager to be near Jesus. They had heard about His exploits and wanted to know more. The party was private, so it seems likely that the woman with the bad reputation crashed it. I can't imagine that the host would have invited her to be the center of attention, especially in a day when women were expected to speak only when spoken to.

Actually, there is no record that the woman said a word, but her actions practically screamed. Luke says that "she came there with an alabaster jar of perfume" (Luke 7:37, NIV). This would have been her most precious possession—a flask of very expensive oil. Obviously, she was up to something. There's another interesting detail in this story: it seems that most of the men at the dinner knew the woman. Why in the world did they know a woman who lived on life's clearance rack?

Can you picture the scene? The woman wasted no time in accomplishing what she came to do. She "stood at [Jesus'] feet behind Him weeping; and she began to wash His feet with her tears, and wiped them with the hair of her head; and she kissed His feet and anointed them with the fragrant oil" (v. 38). As she poured out her precious gift on Jesus' feet, perfume filled the place, and all eyes were fixed on Jesus and a woman of ill repute.

The men who came to rub elbows with Jesus watched His attention shift from them to someone they considered unworthy. Simon, the Pharisee hosting the dinner, was embarrassed that Jesus would allow such a sinful woman to engage Him. She did not kneel and ask for forgiveness of her sins. She simply wept, overcome with emotion, and lavished her attention on her Lord. Simon silently judged her actions and questioned Jesus' character for allowing her to touch

Him. Jesus knew what he was thinking and challenged his judgmental assumptions.

> Do you see this woman? I came into your house. You did not give me any water for my feet, but she wet my feet with her tears and wiped them with her hair. You did not give me a kiss, but this woman, from the time I entered, has not stopped kissing my feet. You did not put oil on my head, but she has poured perfume on my feet.
>
> —LUKE 7:44–46, NIV

It was the custom in that day to have water ready so your guests could wash the dust from their feet. However, Simon had not provided water for Jesus' feet. Nor had he anointed Jesus' head with oil. It is obvious that although Simon had invited Jesus to dine at his home, he did not understand who Jesus was.

Jesus let Simon know how highly He valued the woman's actions. According to Mark 14:5, the ointment was worth about three hundred denarii, which was more than a year's wages. It was most likely the greatest material sacrifice she could have given and must have been her life's savings. However, she was not worried about the money. She wanted to give it to her Lord, and she wanted what only He could give her—forgiveness.

> "Therefore, I tell you, her many sins have been forgiven—as her great love has shown. But whoever has been forgiven little loves little." Then Jesus said to her, "Your sins are forgiven."
>
> —LUKE 7:47–48, NIV

This bold woman is a great example of the love that our Lord has for each of us. She is unnamed so everyone can relate to her story. The details of her life might be totally unlike the challenges you have faced. Yet that doesn't matter. Jesus can turn anyone's scars into stars. Who cares what people have to say about you? Let them talk about your failures. So what! Their words cannot prevent what God has planned for you. Ignore them. Don't let your past talk you out of your future!

Here's the question I would like you to honestly ask yourself: "What am I waiting on?"

We often say we are waiting on God. However, God is waiting on us. We have already been designed by Him for roles that only we can fulfill. The woman who anointed Jesus' feet played her part. She could not have known that we would be reading and discussing her victorious story thousands of years later.

Don't let your past talk you out of your future!

The unnamed woman acted in spite of the opposition. It's important for you to know that all the forces of darkness cannot stop what God has planned for your life.

Put Failure in Its Place

I know what failure looks like. I have experienced enough wrong decisions to last me a lifetime, yet I am still on my feet and experiencing the greatest time of my life. When I returned to my parents' house with my boys, I felt lame. At thirty-six, it was easy to find reasons for my misery and justify future failures. It would have been easy to write off my dreams, but I realized that the longer I made excuses, the longer I would live a less-than life.

Joel Osteen says that "excuses give us permission to settle for less than God's best." He's exactly right. Everyone has his or her list of excuses: "I can't lose weight—my metabolism is slow. Everybody in my family has this addiction. It's in my genes." That might be true, but you are still not powerless. You can make adjustments that bring change. You were created by God to overcome challenges. But as long as you hang onto your excuses, you will stay in your mess.[1]

"You have to draw the line in the sand" and tell yourself, "That's enough!" Refuse to stay miserable. Dump your excuses.[2] One of the greatest gifts you have from God is tomorrow. You can arise in the morning and know that His faithfulness is new every day. Get off the comparison roller coaster and become the *you* God created you to be. He will give you the greatest revelations of your life.

Repeat this until it sinks into your heart: Nobody can beat you at being you. And nobody can keep you from being you *but you*. Before you can break your addiction, you must trash your excuse for it. You are not a failure as long as you get up one more time than you fall down. Everything you are going through serves a purpose. It's preparing you for where God is taking you.

My family is going through one of the hardest trials that we have ever faced. My dad, our strong patriarch, is now in stage seven of the Alzheimer's process. I can tell you that nothing could have prepared our little family for Alzheimer's. Because my parents have been in ministry for over fifty years, they have spent their lives giving to others. As a vibrant couple who always looked and acted much younger than their ages, they could not have imagined something like this bringing their lives to a screeching halt.

Alzheimer's is a dreaded disease. It affects about 5.8 million people in our nation,[3] and it changes the trajectory of their lives. My parents have traveled countless miles for the gospel. They have been around the world numerous times. Their life plan was to keep traveling and preaching until God was ready for them to enter their eternal home. When asked about retirement, my dad always said that the word *retirement* is not in the Bible. He had no plans to retire. He was an independent force of a man, a pacesetter who had planted churches and spiritually fathered other pastors for years. He was the kind of person who could change the dynamics of a room just by entering it.

But a diagnosis changed everything. Who could imagine that an active sixty-seven-year-old who would rather preach than eat would become an invalid who needs the help of others? Nobody could. But when Alzheimer's showed up, my parents had to decide how they would deal with it. They could easily blame God for not sparing them. They could have fallen into depression and forgotten all about the faith scriptures they had lived by throughout their lives. But they didn't.

I can tell you that this trial has put us all on our knees. Tears flow freely and emotions run high. There is no cure for Alzheimer's. It eventually robs your loved one's mind and nullifies your plans. As my dad's memory deteriorated, there could be no more international travel. And as my mom spent more time taking care of him, she began withdrawing from her commitments. Four and a half years later, Dad is in an advanced stage of this horrendous disease. Once a very active man, he now comes alive about three in the afternoon, when sundowning (confusion and agitation that worsens in the afternoon and evening) kicks in.[4]

I have invited you into my family's inner circle because I want you to understand the changes underway in our lives. When asked, "How is this disease affecting you?" my mom explains that she prays to be conformed to the image of Jesus. My brother and I have called her our hero and let her know that she is a genuine champ. She totally considers Dad's dignity in everything that is done for him, and she goes above and beyond in her care of him.

Maybe things are not working out the way you want because God is working out something better.

This illness has caused my brother and me to look at life through a whole new set of lenses. As my brother assists the nurses in bathing Dad or, in the evening, as I help my mom change him for bed, we are experiencing a new love radiating through our family. This would not have happened without the current tragedy. Daily, we mourn the gradual passing of our family's vibrant leader. The process is slow, so we must stay attuned to God's Word and speak life to every situation that comes.

Did God do this? Absolutely not! This is life. Everyone I know has challenges of some sort. This just happens to be ours, and we will trust God in it. Could Dad be healed? Absolutely! We know for sure that he will be healed ultimately, when God decides. It can happen here on earth or in heaven. But it will happen.

We know for sure that my dad has always trusted the

process. He has always told us that, in every challenge, God is working it all out for our good. So, there is no way we will question the healing Savior in this situation. God's got this! "We know that all things work together for good to those who love God, to those who are the called according to His purpose" (Rom. 8:28).

If you are in a storm, know that God is in it with you. He designed you to meet life's obligations while maintaining a faith stance. The only time life gets unbearable is when you fail to keep your eyes on His promise to work all things for your good. Trust Him. Maybe things are not working out the way you want because God is working out something better.

Testimony

I am a single mom of three children. I have an eight-year-old, a four-year-old and a two-year-old. I was molested as a child by a person very close to me in my family. I was always told that I would never amount to anything. I was told I would not graduate high school and would end up pregnant and dropping out. I got pregnant in my senior year and still graduated high school on time. I was supposed to get married on October 13, 2019. The guy I was marrying was my best friend from childhood. Before the wedding, in August 2019, I realized I was being mentally abused, and I could not put my children through this anymore. I have been saved before as a child but when I got saved in September 2018, I started changing my life around.

Real Talk Kim came to my church at Five Point Church in Easley, South Carolina. Ever since I met her, I knew my life would be different. I have forgiven the person who molested me. I don't even think about it anymore. It used to be stuck in the back of my head, and now I don't even think about it anymore! I have started [watching] *Live at Nine*. I have read *Beautifully Broken*. I am currently reading and going through daily *Beautifully Whole*.

About three weeks ago, I was sitting in my kitchen contemplating killing myself. I had had enough. I thought, "I will never find anybody who will love me and my children without mentally abusing us and who will help me raise them in a godly home." I kept thinking about the breakup, about the wedding coming up that wasn't happening, and then I surrendered it all to God. When I did that, I tell you that I felt the Holy Spirit take everything off of me. I didn't have the urge to commit suicide anymore, I didn't think about the wedding anymore, I didn't think about the breakup anymore, I was happy that God got me out of that before I married this man.

I have prayed to God for a month before we broke up to show me if this was meant to be. He showed me that. He sent me so many signs; He answered me when I prayed to Him and told me to get out of it, to let him go. Real Talk Kim's ministry has blessed my life because she is a true and honest woman of God, and she has been through it. I am so glad that I found her, and that I can do *Live at Nine* with her every night, because it really saved my life. Now I don't even worry anymore; I don't even have any fear anymore, because I gave it all to God. Therefore, I know that He is going to take care of me and my three children. I now have faith that everything is gonna work out because my God is an awesome God.

—M

Today's Declaration

Lord, I decree and declare that I am growing stronger in faith and will reach my full potential. No matter what might try to hold me back, I will push through the door of opportunity that You have opened for me. I am now challenging myself to grow stronger through each storm. I realize that a storm is a season, not a monument. I am the person You called me to be, Lord. When I read Your Word, You impart Your life and restore me, day by day and breath by breath.

CHAPTER 10

No Longer a Victim

THERE IS A moment when you get sick and tired of being the victim in your own story, and you decide to get whole. That is the moment when you quit expecting your loved ones to fix you and you become willing to do what it takes to be healed.

Even though my boys and I moved into my parents' home, I came to realize that nobody could fix me. Expecting anybody to do that would have been unfair. Only I could make the changes I needed to make. I could no longer expect other people to produce the results that would give me happiness.

This change in my thinking was a giant leap. Over the years, my ex-husband and I had relied on my dad to be our Santa Claus. When we needed a car, Dad miraculously produced it. When we needed rent money, I knew whom to call. I guess I thought money was no object to my parents. It was as though I wanted independence but clung to the dependence that temporarily solved my problems. It was only after God healed me that I came to my senses and understood how my parents had charged my debt on their credit cards and even borrowed on their second mortgage. They did whatever was necessary to keep their little girl "happy."

Codependency Is a Big Word

Now we realize that we were all codependent and that my parents were enablers who produced another enabler in me. About fifteen years ago, my mom and her friend established a Celebrate Recovery chapter in their church. It's a program for people dealing with "hurts, habits, and hang-ups."[1] My mom could not have realized at that point that she needed to understand the codependency and enabling in her own family. Yet, as she reached out to the hurting, she learned about us too. She gained knowledge of God's purpose for everyone and saw how it was possible to hold others so close that nobody could grow past his or her own issues. She learned that we must instead grow up in the knowledge of God's plan for each of us.

Because my mom had matured with low self-esteem and insecurity, it was easy for her to become codependent with the broken people in her life. My parents were not born with silver spoons in their mouths or raised in families of more than enough. When my parents were newlyweds, their parents were unable to assist them financially. My parents learned to make it on their own, no matter the cost. Because they were full-time evangelists, their income came only from the churches where they ministered weekly. If they were not in a revival, they had no income. They could not call home and expect a financial blessing. Their parents did not have it to give.

Because they made it through the hard years in their own marriage, my parents did not want their children to go without. It was easier for them to sacrifice luxuries so their kids could be blessed. However, they were enabling me, and it taught me to enable. So, during my marriage, I had no problem making excuses for the poor decisions my husband and I made. I did not realize that I had accepted certain abnormalities as norms. For example, the fact that my eight-year-old boy cooked his own meals when his parents weren't there for him should have alerted me to a problem. And when he *expected* to take care of his hurting mom, I should have realized that I was supposed to be taking care of him, not the other way around.

I mention my son so you can get the bigger picture. When his grandparents gave him a FryDaddy for Christmas because they knew he was the family cook, I should have realized that something was really wrong in our home. I didn't because my husband and I were so broken, in a selfish way. Instead of protecting our children, we made excuses. For example, I protected my image of the man I adored. Not everything he said was right, but I defended every word.

At the time, I was CEO of my own design firm. I worked with very wealthy people every day. My world revolved around name brands, expensive watches, new technology trends, and even my ten-carat diamond. Yet I felt the need to be a people pleaser. I could not see past what should have been my safe place, my happy place, and my home. We looked so well put together, but on the inside we were fragmented.

Then one day, I got it: if you really want someone out of your life, remove yourself. That revelation was the beginning of my life change. It was not easy to follow through. It would have been easier in the short term to stay comfortable in my pain, settle for less, and wait for others to fix me. But it was time to own it. I had to break out of codependency and all aspects of victim mentality.

It's Not Always About What You Did

Codependency and comfort zones are easier only in the short term. Do you remember the Bible story of the man with the withered hand? (See Matthew 12; Mark 3; and Luke 6.) If you had known this man, you probably would have considered him disabled because only one of his hands functioned. I doubt that he daydreamed about being "normal," because being disabled had become his norm. I also doubt that he found a way to fit in with the guys.

Although he could still participate in the community, he had to deal with the shame of his condition. I'm sure he wanted to be like the other people at the synagogue. No doubt, he did whatever he could to fit in, but I'm sure it wasn't enough. He could try to hide his disability by covering it or keeping his hand in his tunic. However, the ruse would have been exhausting and would not work forever.[2]

Can you relate to what this man suffered? Maybe you have two perfectly good hands but still live with shame and self-condemnation. You might blame yourself for things you could not control and could not fix. Millions of people do. Life is just hard sometimes. No one is guaranteed a path strewn with roses. And if you get the roses, they have those nasty thorns. Some marriages are not going to make it. Some companies will not succeed. There are illnesses that doctors cannot heal.

Since my dad was diagnosed with Alzheimer's, I understand the man with the withered hand much better. I can imagine how hard he tried to make things better. I watch my mom juice the best organic veggies and fruits daily so my dad gets the best nutrition. She spends a fortune on vitamins that support brain health. She listens to numerous holistic neurologists telling her how to make him well.

Yet we all know that Dad's healing will come only if the Lord Jesus gives him a miracle. The same was true for the man with the withered hand. Now that my family has walked in his shoes in some way, I understand what it means to have a miracle as your only option.

Jesus Intervenes

> Again he entered the synagogue, and a man was there with a withered hand. And they watched Jesus, to see whether he would heal him on the Sabbath, so that they might accuse him. And he said to the man with the withered hand, "Come here."
>
> —Mark 3:1–3, ESV

We don't always understand how or why we end up in certain places and seasons in our lives. Sometimes, it just happens. We find ourselves in situations we could never imagine for ourselves. I think the man with the withered hand probably grappled with that feeling.[3] Having lived as less than, he realized that change had to happen.

I believe he heard about this man, Jesus, who stood against certain aspects of the religious system. It must have seemed that, ever since Jesus came, change was happening. Maybe that's why the man went to the synagogue that day. He may have heard that Jesus would be there. Who knows? Or maybe his parents encouraged him to try one more thing. What did he have to lose?

Anyway, he was at the synagogue when Jesus showed up on the Sabbath. Can't you just see that room full of Pharisees and other religious people? They already knew that Jesus wasn't afraid to challenge their system, Sabbath or no Sabbath. Now they were waiting to see what Jesus would do about the man with the withered hand.

Of course, Jesus knew what they were thinking. He saw the judgment in people's hearts. So He asked the bystanders, "'Is it lawful on the Sabbath to do good or to do harm, to save life or to kill?' But they were silent. And he looked around at them with anger, grieved at their hardness of heart, and said to the man, 'Stretch out your hand.' He stretched it out, and his hand was restored" (Mark 3:4–5, ESV).

Can you imagine how this hurting man likely felt? It must have been hard for him to stretch out the hand that had caused him so much embarrassment. It must have been hard for him to imagine people seeing him as normal, as no longer the victim in his own story. Yet he pushed past his fears and presented his withered hand to Jesus, and his life changed in an instant.

You will sound like what you listen to most of the time.

That doesn't mean the man never had another problem. Our own experiences tell us that our breakthroughs don't always get rave reviews. Nor do they end all our troubles. But I imagine he much preferred his life after he had been healed and made whole than the one he lived before then.

Like that man, we all have hindrances or pain we hide from others. I often say that life is no joke. Making it through sickness, divorce, or depression is not easy. Just as the man

Testimony

I first want to say how much I truly appreciate your ministry. I can relate to your story in a way I've never related, and I believe God definitely put me in your path. I have been sick and tired of being sick and tired. I googled one day "preaching on letting go." You were the first one that came up. Even though I was listening to messages from months ago, it was as if you were speaking directly to me. I have been stuck for YEARS!!! I was raised [to believe] that divorce was bad, and you were going to hell if you got one. I allowed that man to throw me around like a rag doll, cheat on me, and even get someone else pregnant. After he finalized the divorce (I wouldn't even sign the papers; that's how hard I was holding on), he had me so brainwashed I didn't think I could live without him. We continued a secret relationship for years ending with me telling his new wife about the affair. I then moved on to a new toxic relationship with an alcoholic whom I met while partying. Then I started being convicted and straightening up, as he didn't want to.

We then began fighting. I have thought for the past *fifteen years* that domestic violence was normal. Everyone did it, some public and others behind closed doors. I reached the point that I had a plan to kill myself and realized I had to get out. After our last fight, I left and ran straight back to the first abuser. I felt [that if] I didn't have someone else controlling my life, I couldn't function. I have been so ashamed and embarrassed of this. I haven't told anyone the things that have gone on really and just tried to carry on. I started really praying, and the Lord started shifting my life. He started making it less convenient for my "visits," and finally showed me how unhealthy this is. When I took a survey on domestic violence, I answered yes to every question. That is when I googled and found you.

I work two jobs, so I miss your nine o'clock teachings, but last night, I watched it after work, while bawling. You kept saying, "I don't know why I keep getting off track." I needed to hear every single word you said. I have for years been going in this vicious cycle, and I am done.

Since I discovered you, instead of listening to music at work, I listen to you. I take notes and I'm starting a women's Bible study where we watch one of your videos, then discuss and are vulnerable with each other.

I've always been aware by the Holy Spirit of my situations, but I never knew how to let go. I felt like I couldn't; but you've inspired me and given me hope in a way no one ever has. From the bottom of my heart I thank you for being obedient. My dream is to one day do the same as you. I want

(CONTINUED . . .)

to create a safe haven for women and children who are in situations like I was (those who feel hopeless and trapped), allowing them a safe haven until they can get on their feet. I want to provide counseling and ministry on a working farm, and that is how we cover everything free to them. God will guide me. If this is meant to come to pass, I know He'll do it, but I have to get healing first. You are helping me more than words can even describe to get there! Thank you!

–C

with the withered hand may have felt less than because of the words of others and his own inner voices, we also allow life situations to determine our altitude and attitude.

The voice you hear the most will impact you the most. You will sound like what you listen to most of the time. You can let negative voices direct you, or you can decide to quit being the victim in your story. I cannot call myself an authority on this matter just because I came through a major storm and am still standing. But I can tell you that, because of the blood of Jesus, I am not a victim but a victor. I didn't get healed because of anything I did. Healing came because I connected with the Lord Jesus.

No Pain Wasted

I want to share a profound statement with you. If you get it, it will change your life. *Bad things happen to good people.* When you understand this statement, you realize that being a Christian or a good person does not protect you from life's calamities. Bad things happen to good people because we live in a fallen world. Sin is prevalent because it has been passed down through the generations, ever since the Garden of Eden. Adam and Eve set us up when they disobeyed God and ate the forbidden fruit. They chose what they thought was good. But it was evil, not only for them, but also for their descendants. Now death is promised to each of us. Because Adam and Eve represented all humankind, they brought the curse of pain and death into God's perfect creation.

Understand that God doesn't waste your pain. I've always heard people say, "When life gives you lemons, make lemonade." Your crises can literally put you on your knees. That's a good place to be if you are having a conversation with God. But if you are letting life knock you down and keep you there, you will become a failure. You can be defeated only if you stay down.

God did not intend for the world to be as it is today. He created a perfect world with no death or pain. He did not desire for us to become victims in our own stories. War, child and sex slavery, starvation, earthquakes, and hurricanes are real. But they weren't God's choice. We can get caught up in asking, "How could a good God let bad things happen?" But we are not smart enough to understand the complete answer. Our response is to trust God even when we don't understand. We trust Him because He is good and everything He does is good. "Every good gift and every perfect gift is from above, and comes down from the Father of lights, with whom there is no variation or shadow of turning" (Jas. 1:17).

God is not fickle or shifty. His will for you does not vacillate between good and bad. His heart is true, and His character is above reproach. You can always trust and rely upon Him. Your struggle may be real, but so is your God. No one can promise you an easy life, but I promise that you can be free. God's track record is flawless. Just because you have had to fight some battles does not mean you are defeated. Even when you lose a battle, you haven't lost the war. With God on your side, you are in the majority. You're on the winning side. You have a place in God's kingdom. You are no longer a victim.

Your struggle may be real, but so is your God.

Today's Declaration

Lord, I release any negative, self-defeating thoughts, feelings, and attitudes. I choose to arise. I declare that You are bold and worthy and the center of my joy. I choose to break free from the chains that have kept me bound. I will walk in victory. Thank You that the Holy Spirit infuses me with Your life and wisdom, which strengthen me—body, soul, and spirit—against all fear and disease. My body is the temple of the Holy Spirit, and my cells are graced by Your goodness and power. In Jesus' name, amen.

CHAPTER 11

What I Really Need

SUCCESS WON'T MAKE you happy. Neither will material things. What will make you happy is finding healing and wholeness. When you say goodbye to feelings of inadequacy and move forward in God's plan—that is pure joy.

In chapter 9 we talked about excuses and how we use them to justify our misery. The question is, Do we want to stay miserable, or do we want to break through? I saw a great quote online: "Don't allow what you're going *through* to block what you're going *to*. God is preparing you for something great."[1]

Sometimes the only thing that changes in a situation is you, and that is enough to change everything. It's a choice not to allow anger, depression, anxiety, and unforgiveness to become excuses and determine your altitude. We will always have challenges to overcome. Conflict is everywhere because people are everywhere. We have to work at living in peace. We blame our marriage failures on communication, money, and physical intimacy, but our own emotional issues undermine our relationships. Not everyone feels secure in himself or herself. Not everyone walks in understanding and forgiveness. And not everyone has the courage to be honest.

Sometimes when you are struggling, you need someone to speak the truth in love. A real friend can pinpoint what's happening in your life and help you to understand your pain. Not everyone can do that for you. It takes someone who has invested the time to build a true relationship with you. It must be someone you can trust—a true friend.

I learned that just because you call someone a friend does not mean he or she is a *true* friend. When I lost everything but my boys, all the friends I thought I had were gone. I was able to let go when I realized that those same friends stuck like glue when I was partying and riding the fast train to hell. But when my situation changed, they simply chose to stay behind in my old life. I discovered that sometimes the obstacles you need to remove from your path have first and last names. In other words, they are people. I am so thankful that God intervened and showed me the true picture. If I had stayed on the train to hell with my "friends," I might have lost them anyway—and my precious boys as well.

Sometimes you have to make a decision that will hurt your heart but heal your soul.

Only God could have covered our family with His love and protected us from my unholy decisions. At the time, I had no idea what I needed. My husband and I were two broken people trying to live a normal life. It just wasn't possible. I had to accept that we were living in the consequences of our decisions. There came a point when

I could no longer justify my failures and our failures with excuses.

Choices can be hard. As Trent Shelton said, "Sometimes you have to make a decision that will hurt your heart but heal your soul."[2] When you decide to move forward, God will take you through! His Word says, "Be strong and courageous. Do not be afraid or terrified because of them, for the LORD your God goes with you; he will never leave you nor forsake you" (Deut. 31:6, NIV).

God promises not to leave you, but He also tells you to be strong, courageous, and not intimidated. When you are intimidated, you make excuses for standing back. To move forward, you have to do away with the excuses that keep you stuck in your mess. Knowing your purpose will help you, because a sense of purpose gives you the unction to keep going.

People who are moving forward know they have the power to change their lives because they have the power to change their minds. That doesn't mean they'll never have another bad break. As Joel Osteen said, "We've all had bad breaks. If it was going to keep you from your destiny God would never have permitted it."[3] Remember what Scripture says: "Trust in the LORD with all your heart, and lean not on your own understanding; in all your ways acknowledge Him, and He shall direct your paths" (Prov. 3:5–6). "God will get you where you're supposed to be" because "God has the final say."[4] But will you trust Him?

Sometimes the obstacles you need to remove from your path have first and last names.

You have been hurt and so have I. However, "it's not worth missing your destiny over. It doesn't have to control the rest of your life." It's all about the decisions you make. If you can understand that every day is a gift from God, it will become easier to take your eyes off the past and make positive choices, even in the midst of crises. You see, where you started does not have to limit where you will go. As Osteen has said, "You may have had a rough start but you don't have to have a rough finish."[5]

Honestly, I have to pinch myself sometimes to make sure my current life is real. How in the world could a loser like me be living in a way she never dreamed was possible? I can tell you that making the hard choice to let go of my old life was worth it!

Key to Success

Do you feel lonely, disconnected, and misunderstood? Do you question every step you take and every decision you make? Are you still allowing your past to dominate your present? Then what do you really need to succeed in life?

It's time to stop making excuses and realize that you can have someone in your life—a Savior—who will lead you into righteous living. Just as certain actions can cause catastrophic results, others can change your future for the better. When you accept Jesus Christ as Lord of your life, He gives you peace that you cannot fathom—and you will experience that peace right in the middle of your turmoil.

The truth is that He has been watchful over you ever since you were conceived! Look at what David wrote about God's watchfulness:

> Oh yes, you shaped me first inside, then out; you formed me in my mother's womb. I thank you, High God—you're breathtaking! Body and soul, I am marvelously made. I worship in adoration—what a creation! You know me inside and out, you know every bone in my body; you know exactly how I was made, bit by bit, how I was sculpted from nothing into something. Like an open book, you watched me grow from conception to birth; all the stages of my life were spread out before you, the days of my life all prepared before I'd even lived one day.
>
> —PSALM 139:13–16, MSG

When you look in the mirror, what do you see? Is it a person so fractured by life that you believe you will never succeed? Is your image so distorted by your viewpoint that you can't find anything positive about your hair, eyes, face, or body structure?

Read the selection from Psalm 139 again. In fact, read the whole psalm. We are marvelously made. Our Lord knows us inside and out and still loves and accepts us. He has been with us every minute of our journey from one season to the next. He has seen our worst failures and our greatest exploits. He was in the secret place when we did things against our bodies and sinned against ourselves. You see, the Bible says that when you sin sexually, you sin against your own body. Paul explains this powerfully:

> Flee sexual immorality. Every sin that a man does is outside the body, but he who commits sexual immorality sins against his own body. Or do you not know that your body is the temple of the Holy Spirit who is in you, whom you have from God, and you are not

> your own? For you were bought at a price; therefore glorify God in your body and in your spirit, which are God's.
>
> —1 CORINTHIANS 6:18–20

Sexual sin brings negative physical consequences because it desecrates the temple (the human body) that houses the Holy Spirit. I know the world plays down this important scripture because the world believes that anything goes. If you watch just a few minutes of television or go to the movies, you will see couples sexually involved outside the bonds of holy matrimony. The popular excuse is that everybody does it.

No one ever said that sex between a man and woman doesn't feel good. But the Bible lets us know that sex should be in the context of marriage. Whether it is premarital sex, adultery, or pornography, sexual sin alters our brain function. We were created to have the mind of Christ, but we cannot have His mind when sex is distorting our focus.

Remember, we were made by God to house the Holy Spirit. He told us we were not our own but were bought with a price. That price was Jesus Christ Himself going to the cross so that we could have eternal life. Paul instructed us to glorify God in both body and spirit. We cannot glorify God when we are participating in sexual sin. Thankfully, God has given us the ability to rewire our brains from sexual sins so we will no longer be ruled by the past.[6] That means making a decision to obey Romans 12:2, which says, "Do not be conformed to this world, but be transformed by the renewing of your mind, that you may prove what is that good and acceptable and perfect will of God."

Remember that no matter what happened in the past, you

can rest on the realization that God has your future. You no longer have to be ruled by the decisions you made. You can determine that it's a new day. Take responsibility for being the creation God made, and decide that your life has purpose. Get into God's Word and allow it to become your daily guide. You cannot know God until you know His Word.

After being raised in a pastor's home, I lived thirty-six years without knowing God's Word. When I began my journey of knowing God, I purchased a children's Bible storybook so I could become acquainted with the many characters of the Bible. I did not know about Joshua and the battle of Jericho, David and the giant, Moses and the Red Sea. I could not answer anyone's questions about the Bible text. Being a pastor's daughter did not magically impart that knowledge to me; I needed to wisely decide to get it for myself.

You might feel broken, but you're chosen. Rest. God's got you.

It's been only seven years since I began my journey of seeking to know the Lord. It's as though I have been schooled for many years because He heard my prayer. The Lord began giving me insight into His Word. He even helped me to memorize many scriptures. I know Him in a way I could never have believed. I have found an assurance that, no matter the situation, His Word has the answer.

As you determine that change is coming, you can be confident that God will make "all things work together for good" in your life (Rom. 8:28). You might feel broken, but you're chosen. Rest. God's got you. You will become grounded in courage and strength when you allow His Word to infiltrate you. Remember what He said to Joshua: "Have I not commanded you? Be strong and of good courage; do not be afraid, nor be dismayed, for the LORD your God is with you wherever you go" (Josh. 1:9). You need not be hounded any longer by thoughts of fear and judgment for the things you allowed in the past. You can know that God has covered you and accepted you as His child.

After receiving Jesus Christ as Lord, you are justified in God's eyes. Your sins are not only forgiven but also washed away. God promises that "He will again have compassion on us, and will subdue our iniquities. [He] will cast all our sins into the depths of the sea" (Mic. 7:19). Being freed from judgment gives you the freedom to serve the God who delivered you. Nothing you have ever done can be brought up from God's memory bank once you accept Jesus as your Lord and Savior.

If you find yourself having to tiptoe around others, you're not walking among your tribe. Find your tribe.

This is how you begin to live in a way that pleases God: you accept Jesus as your Lord and Savior. Paul tells us in Colossians 2:13–14 that we were dead because of our sins. That means we were born with a sinful nature. But Jesus' sacrifice made a way for us to overcome that nature. He made forgiveness possible, and His grace empowered us to live holy. Jesus willingly represented every sinner and took on Himself every sin that would ever be committed. He did this as He allowed Himself to be crucified.

> He personally carried our sins in His body on the cross [willingly offering Himself on it, as on an altar of sacrifice], so that we might die to sin [becoming

> immune from the penalty and power of sin] and live for righteousness; for by His wounds you [who believe] have been healed.
>
> —1 PETER 2:24, AMP

Reaping, Sowing, and Relationship

When responding to God's call on your life, it is important to understand that He meets you where you are, not where you pretend to be. Sometimes, even after you decide that it's time for change, your circumstances don't change. You are responsible for how long you allow whatever hurt you to haunt you. After you decide that you are ready to move forward, release the hurt to God so He can heal you. You cannot change the people in your life. You can only decide how you and your life will change.

You also need to know whether you are with your tribe. If you find yourself having to tiptoe around others, you're not walking among your tribe. Find your tribe. Don't waste time on people who don't have your back but flee the moment a crisis hits. All of us have gone through, are going through, or will go through crises. It's a given. It's so important to be linked with those who will hold your hand when you need a hand to hold.

As our family walks through my dad's illness, I am seeing the reality of reaping and sowing being manifested day by day. People from our past are volunteering to sit with Dad for periods of time so Mom can get a break. This is a realization of God's promise to be there when we need Him. You see, my parents have gone above and beyond to help others throughout the years, even when they might have been tempted to quit. But God said, "Do not be deceived, God is not mocked; for whatever a man sows, that he will also reap" (Gal. 6:7). My parents are seeing firsthand that when you give to others, God's promise comes to pass.

With elevation comes separation from all things that cause contamination.

When we read Galatians 6:7, we tend to fear that all the bad things we have done will come back to haunt us. We need to also see the verse from another angle: when we do good for others, we will reap from our good works. Those you have helped might not be the ones who return to bless you, but God will send strangers if necessary. I know from experience that God can even send total strangers to become your best friends.

You don't have to walk alone. If loneliness has been your constant companion, it's time to start trusting what God is doing. Sometimes, He moves people out of your life to make room for the tried-and-true companions who are on the way. If you want change, you have to expect change. With elevation comes separation from all things that cause contamination. Wrong relationships can delay your purpose. When you tolerate unhealthy friendships, you tolerate delay. Don't do it! You are on your way to a new day. Let God put you where you need to be. The better you become, the

Testimony

I've been in and out of abusive relationships. The last one [just] about took me out. Since I've been following RTK, I've gotten honest with myself, healed the hurt little girl that was abused as a child, forgiven my exes that abused me. Now I've changed the patterns that kept me stuck for so long. I can live again. I do your *Live at Nine* and Inner Circle. What a blessing.

–C

better you will attract. It's like finding the right shoe; if someone is meant for you, he or she will fit perfectly, with no forcing, no struggling, and no pain.

When you have made Jesus the Lord of your life, you will be amazed by how He creates the shift that sets up your new beginning. You'll discover that the things you used to need mean nothing to you now. You will see life through different eyes and experience it with a different heart. What once hurt you will now bless you. What once drove your bad decisions will now inspire wise ones. Watch how God creates beauty from ashes.

What once hurt you will now bless you. Watch how God creates beauty from ashes.

Trust the process. Everything is coming together for your greater good. Jesus Christ is all you need. He will lead, guide, and direct you into all truth. And He will lead you into the life you long to live.

Testimony

I am forty-seven years old, a mother of three wonderful kids, and married three times and divorced twice. The beginning of this year [I] was going on divorce number three. I am an emotional "runner." When things don't go my way and things get tough, I'll just pack up and leave. In February, I saw Kim at a revival at our church, and God started doing a work on me. By March, we were in marriage counseling, and then just two months ago, God changed my heart in a mighty way. As I listen to Real Talk Kim on *Live at Nine* and work on the studies in the Inner Circle, God is changing, rearranging, and reclaiming me. I no longer am "stuck like Chuck." I have surrendered all and am ready to live life to the fullest that God has for me. Thank you, Kim, for your inspiration, love, and encouragement daily to bring this broken woman to the best part of my life. Love you!

—R

Today's Declaration

I decree and declare that I choose the gift of today. I choose to focus on the blessings in my life. Nothing will steal my joy—no hurts, habits, or hang-ups will steal my peace. Lord, keep me close to You, because I trust Your process. I declare that all things are working for my good. Lord, I open my heart to Your power and love. I invite You to touch every area of my life, in the name of Jesus Christ.

CHAPTER 12

Free to Be Me

NOBODY IS BETTER at being you than *you*. Nobody else has your calling, and no one can do what you do like you can. Your job is to find yourself and be unapologetically *you*. You know by now that I was a prime example of trying to live in other people's shadows and walk in other people's shoes. My biggest regret is that finding myself took so many years, because once I did, I found contentment, joy, and a life of bringing hope to others—a life beyond anything I could have dreamed.

By the time I returned to my parents' home with my boys in tow, I had lost my identity. I had no idea where to find the marvelously created woman Psalm 139 described. Bad as things were, my parents were one of my greatest assets. They believed in me when I didn't believe in myself, and they helped me to take positive steps. For one thing, my dad let me know that if I was going to live under his roof, I would be at church every service and would join the worship team.

I hated the idea of being in an all-white congregation, but I got my dad's point. My parents had begun pastoring this small congregation only about a year before I arrived. Before that, the church had been through so much upheaval that all the leaders left, and so did most of the congregation. Because my parents' former church had planted this one, my dad knew it was his responsibility to revive what had been lost. He could not have known that I would be coming home in need of revival myself. I had worked hard to keep my troubles hidden from my parents. I allowed them inside my world only when things got too rocky for me to handle myself. That's when I would pull back the curtain just a little and give them a peek at what was going on. Only years later would I tell them the whole sordid story.

The Wisdom to Find Yourself

When I began to find the real me, I came out of hiding and learned to conquer the judgmental voices that had been telling me (for years) that I could not accomplish anything. It was a big step forward, but the little girl with the learning disability was still trying to rule me, even though I was turning thirty-seven.

Don't ask me why I decided to host a women's conference after being home just two years. I don't know the answer. I just know that women began coming alongside me to assist in any endeavor I would undertake. My mom was the head of my cheerleading squad, making all the flyers and even designing a logo when I decided my ministry would be called Conquering Hell in High Heels. (You can read in chapter 8 about how a poem from my son

What God is preparing for you is worth the wait.

gave me that name.) The name stuck, so I decided it was time to host the conference. The hilarious thing is that I did not preach. I asked my mom, sister-in-law, and other friends to preach because I knew they would deliver my heart. I did not preach at the following year's conference either. Yet several hundred women registered and attended.

I came to realize that I was an influencer and could do what I never dreamed I could do. Really, the four-year-old me knew me better than the thirty-something me did. As a little girl, I knew in my heart that I wanted to preach. Now I was being given the opportunity. It was time to step up to the plate and take a swing at the ball.

When I felt I was ready, I approached my dad, who was my pastor, about preaching on Sunday. Of course, he was a seasoned pastor and had been in ministry most of his life. He knew I wasn't quite ready, but he gave me a chance to grow. As I preached, I came up with the strangest sayings, and he would reprimand me when we got home. He explained that some things just can't be said in the pulpit.

If you know me, you know that I make some statements that shock even me. Looking back, I'm thankful that when I thought I was ready to preach, I listened to those who were seasoned in ministry and could help me learn. Without that guidance, I could have fallen flat on my face. Had I ignored their wisdom, I could have ended up like a shooting star.

What God had prepared for me was worth the wait. What God is preparing for you is worth the wait. Be thankful for the pastors and others who love you enough to be honest with you as you make your way toward your destiny.

Change and the Look of Success

Because I called my ministry Conquering Hell in High Heels, you probably envision me stepping onto the platform in stilettos. I did for a season, until I just couldn't handle it anymore. It was hard to keep my thoughts together when my feet were screaming louder than my voice. They were killing me! Eventually, I decided that I needed comfort more than I needed style.

I thank God that, by this time, I had fallen in love with the woman He made me to be. I no longer needed to live by comparing myself with others. I wasn't trying to measure up to them anymore. I had found myself. What a great revelation it was! It totally saved my life.

Then I discovered Doc Martens—one of the most comfortable boots I have ever worn. I found them in all colors and decided they were made for me. It did not matter whether I was wearing a dress or jeans; those boots completed my style. As strange as my style was, it did not stop there. I also became acquainted with tutus. If you enter my garage today, you will see tutus of every color hanging in a corner. For several years, no one saw me in anything but tutus and Doc Martens. I would dress up in my outfit of choice and feel like I was ready for the catwalk. I refused to allow anyone to talk me out of what God revealed as being *me*. I now know that I was created to be different. I do not pattern myself after anyone, and I don't know anyone who is like me.

Each day, I walk into a deeper revelation of the woman God is creating within me. I am now CEO of a reputable ministry and know that God is opening doors that no one can close. I have watched Him open the windows of heaven and pour out blessings on me that only He could have given. It reminds me of His promise from the third chapter of Malachi:

> "Bring all the tithes into the storehouse so there will be enough food in my Temple. If you do," says the LORD of Heaven's Armies, "I will open the windows of heaven for you. I will pour out a blessing so great you won't have enough room to take it in! Try it! Put me to the test!"
>
> —MALACHI 3:10, NLT

Remember: I was the woman who came home broken, with no income. Now God has totally restored everything the devil stole from me throughout my lifetime. Learning Malachi 3:10 was part of my transformation. It tells us to put God to the test, and He will pour out blessings that we cannot contain. This can happen only when we pay our tithes into the storehouse. (The storehouse is whatever church you attend. That is the place where you are fed and covered.)

May I tell you something? I did not understand tithing when I returned to my parents' home. My dad graciously let me know that I could not be blessed as long as I kept robbing God by withholding my tithe (a tenth of my income) from Him. Dad let me know how paying ten cents of every dollar would take the curse off my money and I would see innumerable blessings. I had a really hard time understanding the concept. At the time, I was making twelve dollars an hour (after I lost my company and was working in retail). I could not understand how my little bit of money could ever help the kingdom of God.

One day, as my sons and I traveled home from Florida, I

took the exit ramp toward a small town near my home. The police had stopped a vehicle on the side of the road, so I cautiously drove past. Immediately, one of the police cars started following me and ordered me to pull over. I knew I wasn't speeding. I was careful to do whatever was necessary to keep the law, but the policeman told me I had broken the law. I was flabbergasted and asked him what I had done wrong. He said that a new law had begun that day called the Move Over Law. It means that if you see a policeman stopped, you must change lanes and proceed cautiously. I had no idea that such a law existed, but that did not matter. I still got a ticket, with a fine of over five hundred dollars. I was sick over it.

When I got to my parents' house, I immediately gave them the bad news. My dad gently said, "Kimberly, I've told you that if you don't pay your tithe, it will be as though your money is in a bag full of holes. You will continually pay out for the unexpected."

I decided to give Malachi 3:10 a try and began paying my tithe each week. I know now that paying my tithe wasn't helping the church as much as it was helping me. I was learning how to give up and let God be God in my life. Money could not be my idol any longer. I had to release it so God could bless me. Thank God, I finally got it! I can tell you that I am abundantly blessed and that money means nothing to me. I receive more than I could ever give, and I never worry about making ends meet.

The lesson of tithing was critical to my transformation. It's another example of not letting my past mistakes dictate my current and future decisions. I allow God to be Lord of my life. I pay my tithes, and I live a life of expectancy. Daily, I expect breakthrough, blessing, success, and health. I feel so free at this time in my life that I love giving to others out of my blessings. That is why I am on social media every day, telling people what God has done for me. How could I not give away what He has given me? It's like a fantasy. My life is better than I could have imagined, and I'm not talking about material things. I'm talking about being able to love thousands on the social media platforms. I really did not know how to love until I experienced total failure. I had no idea how to forgive until I was forgiven by God. Now I can walk in forgiveness toward all who contributed to my downfall. And each day, I forgive myself for all the things I allowed to touch my life. I am determined to reach as many people as possible for the cause of Christ. There is no way I could ever pay back all that I have been given.

Keep On Keeping On

When you are ready for a life change, God is ready for you. He will never force it on you. But He will stick with you. He never leaves you. It's hard to understand or imagine how He could love you even when you are unlovable. Yet He does.

I'm sharing this because when you release your past and move forward, it's as though you shed layer upon layer upon layer of past mistakes and hurts. At times, you forgive those who have hurt you, yet the pain seems to resurface. I understand that. I have been there. Rejection used to determine my actions. Now I know that forgiving today does not necessarily mean that I won't have to forgive again tomorrow. Forgiveness is a daily thing.

The most amazing feeling is when you consciously forgive

someone. Suddenly, you can see the person who sold you out or hurt or deceived you in some other way, and you no longer feel your heart beating out of your chest. The sight of that person no longer causes anxiety attacks. The pain of what he or she did doesn't overwhelm you anymore. The change isn't always immediate. That's why you may need to forgive again and again.

I think this is one reason so many people quit church. They get hurt by someone's opinions or judgments, and they allow the hurt to determine their choices going forward. If you can understand that church is filled with imperfect people, it will be easier to understand when someone offends you. You will accept the fact that there are no "angels" in the body of Christ. We are all flawed, and we all need forgiveness.

Thank God that He knows us intimately and can understand us when we fall. It's not about falling anyway. It's about getting up again and again and again.

Choose Your Bird

Have you ever heard about how eagles soar above the storms, but chickens scratch in the dirt for their food? Joyce Meyer talks about the differences between the two birds. She explains that eagles are powerful, perching and soaring high up, spying out prey with their sharp vision. Like eagles, chickens also "have wings and feathers and beaks," but they live very differently from eagles. When a storm approaches, the chicken clucks and runs for cover, while the eagle turns its "face into the storm" and flies straight into it when the time is right. "He'll catch the violent updrafts caused by the storm and be immediately swept up above the clouds and into the bright sunshine." While the chicken huddles with its frightened friends, the eagle chooses to "remain above the clouds until the storm blows over."[1]

You'd better believe I would rather be identified with the eagle than the chicken! What about you? How do you act when you receive a bad diagnosis? When your job is in jeopardy? When your family is in upheaval? Do you immediately start worrying about the what-ifs? Or are you like the eagle that uses the storm to its advantage?

I can tell you that God has called you to be an eagle. Meyer quotes Isaiah about this, and it is the perfect scripture. It says that "those who wait on the LORD shall renew their strength; they shall mount up with wings like eagles, they shall run and not be weary, they shall walk and not faint" (Isa. 40:31).

The eagle understands its identity and then lives the way it was created to live. The greatest day in your life is the day you become acquainted with the *you* God created you to be. You might not be there yet, but it's in the silent seasons that you will begin to see it. In fact, you cannot have any idea how resilient you really are until you have been rejected. You can't know your strength until it's tested by pain. You cannot really succeed until you go through challenges and overcome them.

The enemy doesn't rob empty vaults.

Then, suddenly, the day comes when you quit trying to make things right with people who won't take ownership of the pain that they cause you. You tell yourself, "It's enough!

I can love them from a distance." That's when you move them out of your VIP section and into your balcony.

The enemy is hoping you will respond to storms like a chicken does. But if he comes calling to intimidate you and bring up your past, it's an indication of something great in your future that he doesn't want you to see. The enemy doesn't rob empty vaults. He's betting that if he can wear you out, the future God promised you will never come to fruition.

The shame is that the enemy often sees more in us than we see in ourselves. I can tell you that, until I let go of the counterfeits who sucked the life out of me, I had no idea that God had created within me a nation shifter. I was letting my situation cloud my present so much that I could not see my future. I learned that you must become friends with your today before you can step into your tomorrow.

Too many people are racing through the present, afraid to face their decisions yet expecting the future to be better. Something is wrong with that picture. The

Testimony

I haven't been on my journey with God for very long. I started listening to Pastor Kim in late August, after I was warned for the third time by God to get my life straight. I had a "numb spirit" as RTK says. I felt nothing for my life, and I was just living day by day while fighting God to keep my unholy lifestyle. But God is an exceptional fighter, and He delivered me. RTK has saved my life through her words given to her by the Lord. Everything she says resonates within me and inspires me to be a better mother, wife, daughter, and granddaughter. I'm forever grateful that God provided me with the ability to hear and finally be able to grasp all the things I needed to understand through Pastor Kim. I have come so far all because of the huge social media platform for RTK. I was baptized October 13, 2019, and I am now living for the Lord 100 percent.

–M

only way to create a better tomorrow is to make good decisions today—yes, even in the midst of the storm.

You have a promise for your life, but certain things can temporarily block your access. Let me explain with an analogy. Because I am a frequent flier, I have learned the importance of weighing my baggage before I leave for the airport. I learned this lesson when I had to shift clothing from an overweight bag to another bag, in public.

The weight of my heavy bag hindered me. In life, you can be so weighed down by the things you allow that you are unable to fly above your circumstances. Everyone around you seems to be succeeding while you keep scratching around in the dirt, with no hope of success.

> *Testimony*
>
> Real Talk Ministry has blessed my life in so many ways. I now have the strength to get up and keep pushing and fighting the good fight for the Lord. I have learned how to stay in my Bible even more now, have more patience, and wait on God more. I truly thank God for Pastor Kim. Love you!
>
> –T

It's time to become the eagle God created you to be. But just because God spoke something into your life doesn't mean it's going to happen. Look at what the writer of Hebrews said:

> Therefore we also, since we are surrounded by so great a cloud of witnesses, let us lay aside every weight, and the sin which so easily ensnares us, and let us run with endurance the race that is set before us.
>
> —HEBREWS 12:1

We have a race to run, but we let excess baggage hinder us. In my experience, many people miss walking in their destinies because they lack the character to press in or are too lazy to seek God for His will. They are so bogged down with unimportant things that they lack the focus and determination to thrive.

Please understand that to become the *me* that God created, I had to pull myself away from my previous life and allow God to remake me. I gave Him permission to rewire the selfish woman who had lived life outside His protection so she could become a whole person who was ready to obey His voice. Had I not done this, nothing from my old life would have changed.

You are free to be you. God has already given you permission. But you must allow Him to be God in every area of your life. It's time to make that choice. Are you ready?

Today's Declaration

Lord, I decree and declare that I will allow You to be Lord of every area of my life. I choose to trust You as You help me to rise above my circumstances. I give You permission to make me into the person You purposed that I would be. I am called, qualified, and chosen. I am a child of God and the apple of Your eye. Your name is my strong tower. As Your child, I can run into it and be safe. By Your Spirit I receive the wisdom I need to conduct my life according to Your ways.

CHAPTER 13

Perfect Just the Way I Am

SOMETHING BEAUTIFUL HAPPENS when God heals you. You start embracing every part of yourself, knowing that God created you perfectly. You accept your uniqueness and you celebrate it. You are content because you have found your lane, and you know that it's yours. When that happens, there is no stopping you.

Of course, you always have choices to make. Few things in life are neutral. Everything you do, say, see, or hear either "lifes" you or "deaths" you. You have to choose who will determine your path: Will you allow God to be Lord of your life? Or will the god of this world guide your steps?

I faced that crossroads and finally decided to live life to its fullest, according to God's plan for me. That opened a whole new realm of decision-making, and it changed how I process each decision I make. I now refuse to let life get me down. Do I have bad days? Yes. I still get the bad with the good, just like you. But it's up to me to awaken each morning and determine what my life will look like. I'm not saying that making choices can keep me from all future crises. Instead, when crises come, I have to *decide* to turn them over to the One who orders my steps.

I refuse to focus on circumstances I cannot change. You need to do the same. There will always be people and things opposing you on your journey. You cannot change them without God's intervention. If you really think you are capable of warring with life on a daily basis, you will soon discover that you are not. You will only become weary and lose your focus on Jesus Christ.

When you realize that you were created as one of a kind, you will find it easier to handle situations whether you come out a winner or a loser. Some battles you won't win—not because you are a failure but because life is tough. Yet, even when you lose the battle, God assists you in winning the war. If you will give it to Him and allow Him to take over, facing the opposition will be much easier.

I know that sounds simple, but it's really profound, as I learned firsthand. Because of my life experiences, I knew how to fight physically, mentally, and emotionally but not with God fighting for me. Now I've learned that, with Him, every decision I make becomes a success. Even when I don't reach the winner's circle, I still win because every good and perfect gift comes from the Father above. (See James 1:17.) Even when I seem to fail, I come out a winner in the long run. With God on my side, I am always in the majority.

Always Asking Why

Our family has a friend who has been very close to us for forty-eight years. When my parents were starting out in marriage and ministry, this man's family was like family to us. He and his wife became the mentors my parents needed as they traveled throughout the United States as full-time evangelists, with my brother and me in tow. Their family became our pattern for success. We watched them pastor growing churches and raise their children to be balanced, even in a pastor's home.

This year, our friend lost his son to a massive heart attack. We were all devastated by the news, especially because our friend had also lost his wife to cancer just eight months earlier. During the grieving process, we all tried to understand why such tragedy had befallen our friend. Our friend cannot understand why his wonderful son died so young, but he also knows that God is too good to do us wrong and too wise to make a mistake.

We looked to the Word and found that David, who became Israel's king, often asked the question *why* in the Book of Psalms. Yet look what God said about David:

> When He [God] had removed him [Saul], He raised up for them David as king, to whom also He gave testimony and said, "I have found David the son of Jesse, *a man after My own heart, who will do all My will.*"
>
> —Acts 13:22

My family and our friend were not the first to struggle with the *whys*. I think the biggest room in the human mind should be dedicated to things we don't understand. I always wondered why bad things happened to me. I used to ask, "Why in the world is my brother so balanced and such a blessing to my parents when I seem to have nothing to offer them but problems? Why am I always having to work hard just to make ends meet? Why couldn't I choose someone who would love me for me? Why, Lord, am I so broken?"

These were the issues I continually processed in my mind as I tried navigating two failed marriages and other issues. I now realize that I lacked any idea about who God had created me to be. The very reason I can now love thousands of people I know only as thumbnails on social media is because an inner transformation changed me from the inside out and allowed me to love myself as I am. I love my funky dressing, my ratchet language, and even my clumsiness. I know I will never be a model, yet I feel beautiful as I walk out to deliver God's Word.

I realize now that life happens in the heat of battle. In that heat we ask questions and make choices that can define our outcomes for generations to come. We cannot act wisely and set ourselves up for success until we first decide that, even when we don't understand them, God's ways are higher than ours. God Himself said, "As the heavens are higher than the earth, so are My ways higher than your ways, and My thoughts than your thoughts" (Isa. 55:9).

His ways and thoughts *are* higher than yours, but they are not unknowable. You can learn what He thinks. I can tell you that when I figured that out, it changed my life. When you understand that God restores lost opportunities and wasted years, you can decide which changes you want to see. It's all about making choices and understanding that God knew you before your parents ever thought about having a child.

I can also tell you that knowing His ways is not enough. We must *do* His ways. I have committed myself to becoming the best preacher that I can be in this life. I also want to be a better wife, mother, sister, and friend. I remember what it felt like to look in the mirror and see nothing but loss, pain, judgment, and loneliness when everyone around me seemed to be making a difference. *But God!* Now I feel love in a way that I had never experienced.

Part of love is choosing to be your best in spite of other people's actions. Love happens when what you want is not important. Love is considering others and their needs. Love is Jesus Christ. He is the true meaning and embodiment of love. Love happens when you know that Jesus *knows* you.

Scripture says that "the eyes of the LORD range throughout the earth to strengthen those whose hearts are fully committed to him" (2 Chron. 16:9, NIV). This beautiful scripture has soothed my aching heart more times than I can count. It is life changing to realize that the Lord knows me when I'm at my high points and when I'm low. He never judges me for the decisions I make but remains my constant help in times of need.

I can remember when I was little and my parents took my brother and me to a small town in north Georgia that resembled a German village. It was built to lure tourists from Atlanta, so it had many fun attractions, like fudge making, Christmas shops, and glassblowers. I was always intrigued by the man who could turn a small glob of liquid into a piano or a bird. I loved watching him blow a molten bubble on the end of his long blowpipe. He then molded the object carefully while keeping it hot in the furnace. If he lost his focus for a moment or if the glass cooled down before the process was finished, the item could be ruined. Sometimes he had to heat it and make it pliable again. It was very tedious and time-consuming work, but I could have watched him doing it all day.

As I rehearse the experience in my mind, I realize that glass-blowing is a lot like the process of becoming spiritually mature. We have to stay in the "oven" for a certain period of time. If we stay there too long or come out too soon, the process fails. It reminds me of the refiner's fire described in Malachi 3:3: "He will sit as a refiner and a purifier of silver; He will purify the sons of Levi, and purge them as gold and silver, that they may offer to the LORD an offering in righteousness."

Each of us is going through the refining process. God calls us to yield to His plan so we can be transformed into His image and likeness. That is how He perfects us. "Whom He foreknew, He also predestined to be conformed to the image of His Son, that He might be the firstborn among many brethren" (Rom. 8:29). The more we see ourselves as Christ sees us, the better we are able to submit to the process and let Him continue His work in and through us.

Call, Purpose, and Purification

God is calling us to be more Christlike. Once we give Him permission (by surrendering our lives to Him), He continues our purification. This is a good thing, but it can be unpleasant and even painful. Without God's grace I would have called it quits many times. I did not like the pain of abandonment and emotional abuse. Yet, in the midst of my pain, I cried out for God to change me. The truth is, when everything was going great, I was too busy and "satisfied" to think that I even needed God.

Paul understood the process of purification much better

than I did. He wrote in Romans 8:18 that "the sufferings of this present time are not worthy to be compared with the glory which shall be revealed in us." The process starts with Jesus Christ, the One who suffered for us, being our Lord. Paul understood that our suffering was also part of the process. Purification can happen in the midst of divorce, adultery, financial failure, or some other challenge. We cannot choose the situations that cause us to come forth as pure gold. We know only that there is a process and that it plays out through difficulty.

Stop being stuck on the struggle!

Difficulty is not your whole life, however. Stop being stuck on the struggle! If all you see is how big your problem is, you will lose sight of who God is and what His plan looks like. Jesus is inviting you to become more like Him. He will not force you. It is His will for you to become pure, but it will not happen until you yield to Him—first by accepting that He came as a sacrifice for you, then by submitting to the refiner's fire.

Paul told us to "cleanse ourselves from all filthiness of the flesh and spirit, perfecting holiness in the fear of God" (2 Cor. 7:1). Again, God never forces Himself or His will on us. He beckons us to change and advances that change only when we invite Him in. If we are faithful to do that, He will finish the work.

Like the glassblower who keeps his eye on his prize until it is completed, we must keep our eyes on being filled with the Holy Spirit. He is our prize. We cannot allow other people's questions or demands to interrupt His flow. We were created for a purpose, to be a picture of perfection, not because we are perfect in ourselves but because God's creative work in us is perfect, even when we are broken. And when it seems like God isn't working in our lives or has forgotten us, we can and must trust in His unfailing love. He is with us.

Life Is Full of Choices

One of the most important things I can tell you again and again is that trials will come. Situations will turn your world upside down. People will hurt you. It's part of the process. You get to decide whether the process will make you or break you. Only you can choose to let the refiner's fire transform you into the image of Jesus Christ. Begin by confessing that you cannot do it alone. You must have the Lord Jesus as your pilot. Give up and allow Him to begin the transformation process.

Stop venting and start praying. You don't need sympathy. You need strength.

Transformation is not a tweak. It's a 360-degree makeover. I am a great example of what transformation looks like. I am absolutely nothing like I was before my encounter with the Lord at the age of thirty-eight. Remember that even after I returned to my parents' home at the age of thirty-six, I did not allow the transformation process to begin in earnest. If I had it to do over again, I would quit rebelling sooner and allow Him to be my Lord sooner. Who knows where I might have been if I had surrendered right away? Yet I am so amazed at my life today that I won't quibble over the timing. I was just a human being who wanted to live one way but lived another, and I'm not the only one. Paul described that tendency in Romans chapter 7:

> What I am doing, I do not understand. For what I will to do, that I do not practice; but what I hate, that I do. If, then, I do what I will not to do, I agree with the law that it is good. But now, it is no longer I who do it, but sin that dwells in me. For I know that in me (that is, in my flesh) nothing good dwells; for to will is present with me, but how to perform what is good I do not find. For the good that I will to do, I do not do; but the evil I will not to do, that I practice. Now if I do what I will not to do, it is no longer I who do it, but sin that dwells in me.
>
> —Romans 7:15–20

Paul wrote more New Testament books than any other writer. He was the most educated pastor, yet he let us know that he had a tough time just being good. He confessed that his sin nature was always warring with his reborn spirit. Thankfully, God sent His Son, Jesus, as a sacrifice for Paul and for us! None of us could have become sinless on our own. Yet here we are, living day by day, full of the Holy Spirit power that raised Jesus Christ from the dead!

A lot of things broke my heart but fixed my vision.

It's important to realize that you have this power to be set free, to release the chains that have bound you most of your life, to give away what has been given to you. That power is love. God's love has made you free. Stop venting and start praying.

You don't need sympathy. You need strength. The storm you are facing may not be a storm at all but a transition.

Sometimes, the only way for God to show you He's in control is to allow situations you cannot control. They teach you that you can go through trials, temptations, sicknesses, and failures but remain standing. They have certainly taught me that much and more. A lot of things broke my heart but fixed my vision.

You are not in the stands watching the game of life; you are on the playing field, where some kind of battle is always underway. No place is more dangerous for those who are disengaged and unaware that the battle is on. But when you recognize this reality, you need to know that you are more than a conqueror through Christ Jesus who loved you. Greater is the One who lives inside you than any situation or environment that might try to suffocate you. (See Romans 8:37 and 1 John 4:4.)

Someday you'll look back on the toughest period in your life and be glad you didn't give up. Once you accept Jesus as Lord, you are no longer obligated to let malice, deceit, anxiety, or depression rule and reign in your life. Everything can change with a decision to live above the fray. That's how you become full of His presence—the same presence that created the world. A decision is the start of being filled with His perfection.

So, exactly how do you decide? You "let the word of Christ dwell in you richly in all wisdom, teaching and admonishing one another in psalms and hymns and spiritual songs, singing with grace in your hearts to the Lord" (Col. 3:16). Paul is saying that you can allow the word of Christ to dwell and overflow in you. You can become strong enough to stand against any force that tries to come against you. You can always believe in you because of the God who created you.

In Ephesians chapter 6, Paul spoke of the armor that Roman soldiers wore in battle. He used it to describe how we can be protected on the field of life. The Roman armor "was constructed of strips of iron joined together with hooks or straps" that covered the chest and kept spears and swords from penetrating.[1]

Someday you'll look back on the toughest period in your life and be glad you didn't give up.

Of course, the Romans fought natural wars against flesh-and-blood foes. It is easier to see a natural enemy than a spiritual one. Your enemies are spiritual. Even when you think you are fighting against people, you have to remind yourself that the battle isn't physical, and it isn't between people. It's a skirmish in the devil's all-out war to steal your focus. He will use whomever you will allow to steal your peace and your attention.

So, take Paul's advice to heart:

> Put on the full armor of God, so that you can take your stand against the devil's schemes. For our struggle is not against flesh and blood, but against the rulers, against the authorities, against the powers of this dark world and against the spiritual forces of evil in the heavenly realms.
>
> —EPHESIANS 6:11–12, NIV

We all know that knowledge is power. When you finally have the answer to your problem, the struggle seems easier, even though the problem remains. For example, when you receive a bad medical diagnosis, fear immediately sets in. It's fear of the unknown and the what-ifs. But when the doctor gives you a game plan to wipe out the disease, you feel a sense of relief, even though the disease is still present.

I think Ephesians chapter 6 is our game plan to wipe out the enemy's work in our lives. Paul tells us to stand firm, no matter what obstacles are ahead. He shows how we can be unwavering when the forces of hell come against us. We have to wear our spiritual wardrobe during our times of prayer and meditation:

> Therefore put on the full armor of God, so that when the day of evil comes, you may be able to stand your ground, and after you have done everything, to stand. Stand firm then, with the belt of truth buckled around your

Testimony

Pastor Kim and her husband, Pastor Mark, have really been genuine in my life. They love me, but also, just tell it like it is. I don't have time for sugarcoated words. Give me the meat! Since starting over two years ago and listening to her, I have opened my own spa, bought a house [and] two cars, and helped my kids with college and my grandbabies. I am a country girl from a small town of eight hundred–no college, no business education, two divorces–a "lost everything" kind of life. But one day (thirteen years ago), my ex-husband, who has passed away from drugs, told me I will always live below the poverty level. Well, I'm not! I determined that day I would never let myself get that low and I haven't gone a day hungry or without a bed since he said that. He was very abusive, mentally and physically, but once I broke away, I started living. I thank God daily that I stumbled across one of Pastor Kim's videos on my newsfeed, and I haven't looked back. Thank you both for your obedience to serve God, as it has blessed me.

–S

> waist, with the breastplate of righteousness in place, and with your feet fitted with the readiness that comes from the gospel of peace. In addition to all this, take up the shield of faith, with which you can extinguish all the flaming arrows of the evil one. Take the helmet of salvation and the sword of the Spirit, which is the word of God.
>
> —EPHESIANS 6:13–17, NIV

I can tell you that "dressing" this way is my daily ritual. The belt of truth, the breastplate of righteousness, and the shoes of the gospel of peace give me the spiritual protection I need to win any war. They do the same for you. Dressing spiritually in preparation for the battle is one big reason I spend time in the Word, morning and night.

Paul also tells us to take up our sword, which is the Bible, and the shield, which is our faith. There can be no faith without the Word. I wish I could adequately describe my excitement in learning about Bible characters who withstood every kind of

Testimony

I found RTK at the lowest point in my life. I had just left a fifteen-year toxic relationship. Like Kim, I have two boys that had lost their mama down the unknown hole of depression and despair, and I just wanted to die. Kim and God spoke life into my most broken parts, and I found the Rock at the bottom. Fast-forward three years; I got to meet Kim in person and hear her preach. More healing happened that day and she's just as amazing in person as she is on screen. Now I am blessed to be part of the Inner Circle, and [I'm] learning to be intentional. Kim's mentoring literally is loving hell out of my dark places and giving me tools to function on a level I have never known. Speaking declarations and prayers out loud over myself has been a life changer. Kim is honest and explains we *always* have a choice. Thank You, Jesus, for Kim leaning into healing. I have been blessed beyond measure, and I pray one day I can walk people out of hell too!

–K

trouble for the sake of the gospel of Christ. I wonder how in the world David, Joseph, and Deborah stood and won in the face of such crises. It still amazes me. But it also reminds me that I can do (and am doing) the same thing.

So can you! When you understand that you are no less important to God than any man or woman who has walked this earth and changed his or her world, you have a reason to stand in spite of whatever you are facing. David, Joseph, and Deborah were amazing and unique people. But so are you. No one can do what you do the way that you do it. No one is equipped to accomplish what you will accomplish. No one will ever be able to fulfill your purpose but you.

You are perfect just the way you are. So, go ahead—*be you*.

Today's Declaration

Lord, I decree and declare that I am who You say I am. I will no longer allow life's situations to determine my steps. I was created to serve You, Lord, and I will spend my days doing it to the best of my ability. I am fearfully and wonderfully made, and I will allow You to assist me in becoming the person You purposed me to be. You wrote me in Your book long before I was born. Therefore, I know that You have a plan for me. It is a plan for peace and not evil, to give me a future and a hope. In Jesus' name, amen.

CHAPTER 14

Qualified by God

IT DOES NOT matter who disqualifies you or why. Everybody has some kind of hurt, and hurt people tend to hurt other people. Some of them will say and do things that hurt *you*. Forgive them and move forward. God is at work in you, and He will *finish* the work.

God is so amazing. In the midst of your struggles, He gives you a peek into a better life and then draws you there. When you catch the vision, you realize there's no better place to be than in the purpose for which God qualified you. He doesn't consult your past to decide whether He wants to use you. Everybody has a story, and yours will be a best seller.

At a conference not too long ago, a friend I brought in as a guest speaker opened her sermon by saying, "Real Talk Kim, we will always honor you, because you gave pain a platform." She said that because everyone who knows me knows my story. I have refused to keep skeletons in my closet that can be used as weapons against me. When my mom and I began my first book, we decided together that everything would be told. There would be no surprises later.

I choose to do whatever it takes to walk in my purpose. That simply means allowing God to elevate me in accordance with His plan. Sometimes, that elevation requires separation, as you already know. Remember that the enemy sees who you are in your premature state, so he tries to kill the deliverer within you, even before it is fully revealed. He's after not who you are but who you are going to be. So, just keep chasing after God despite the enemy's attacks.

One of my favorite passages is one I have already quoted, but I feel compelled to quote it again. In it, Paul gives us a beautiful example of goal setting.

> I'm not saying that I have this all together, that I have it made. But I am well on my way, reaching out for Christ, who has so wondrously reached out for me. Friends, don't get me wrong: By no means do I count myself an expert in all of this, but I've got my eye on the goal, where God is beckoning us onward—to Jesus. I'm off and running, and I'm not turning back.
>
> —PHILIPPIANS 3:12–14, MSG

Paul knew about his inconsistencies, faults, and failures. Although he was a powerful leader, a prolific writer, and a church planter, he did not act like he had it all together. I'm sure he was known by all the religious leaders of his day, yet pride did not determine his altitude. If Satan could have convinced Paul that he didn't need God, Satan could have won a great victory. But Paul was determined to keep his eyes on the prize—the goal, which was Jesus Christ. He knew that even in his best state, he could not accomplish his purpose without the Lord. His example warns us not to believe that we are self-sufficient. That lie is how Satan sets us up for failure.

And what about vision? If you don't have a vision for your future, you could easily return to your past. Scripture says, "Where there is no vision, the people perish" (Prov. 29:18, KJV). Without a planned destination, you cannot know where to go. You need a vision and a vision statement to set up your future. It's not a rehearsed statement gleaned from someone else's notes or book but a goal carefully stated after much contemplation and soul-searching. Ask yourself what motivates you to be you. What excites you as you arise each morning to meet another day?

You never have to chase what God has placed within you.

A person without a vision is a person without a future. The writer of this verse, Solomon, understood the importance of having a vision. Some experts say he became king of Israel as a teenager.[1] Whatever his age was, he realized that he lacked the wisdom and knowledge to lead a great nation. So, when God asked him what he wanted, Solomon asked for wisdom and knowledge to rule God's people. God was so impressed with Solomon's humility that He gave him not only the ability to rule Israel but also a wise and understanding heart. God told Solomon that the wisdom and knowledge He gave him would be unlike what any other human being had ever experienced. (See 2 Chronicles 1:7–12.)

In fact, God made Solomon the smartest man who ever lived. No other person in history would ever match his intellect. Just a simple, humble prayer changed Solomon's life and made him one of the wealthiest men who ever lived. I think

God uses this example to show us how important it is to seek Him. It also reveals that you never have to chase what God has placed within you.

Why Seek God?

The greatest change in my life came when I understood the importance of seeking God in my personal life—not for what He could give me, not for financial gain, and not for the knowledge that would propel me into international ministry; I sought Him just to know Him.

We cannot grow spiritually and develop in the Lord without having His knowledge. That is what causes us to grow and mature daily. It takes persistence, so He tells us what to do:

> Ask, and it will be given to you; seek, and you will find; knock, and it will be opened to you. For everyone who asks receives, and he who seeks finds, and to him who knocks it will be opened.
>
> —MATTHEW 7:7–8

This scripture is so simple yet so profound! Matthew directly quoted Jesus Christ, who promised that our asking, seeking, and knocking would produce results.

That is all I need to know. God is impartial and loves every human being the same. He doesn't play favorites. Yet some people seem to get all the blessings. Why? It's a question I hear from so many who are suffering lack in their personal lives. The most important thing I can say in response is that God doesn't make anyone sick or poor. He has given us simple solutions to our struggles—so simple that we think they can't be real.

I can honestly tell you that when I repented after years of struggling and decided to change, He stepped in and changed me, my life, and my surroundings. He also gave me peace in the midst of turmoil. My prayer as you reach this point in this book is that you understand the simplicity and power of the gospel. It doesn't have to be complicated to change your life. It has to be believed and acted upon.

My life today might be considered boring to people who don't understand that I am walking out my purpose. I am no longer the partier or the socializer. I don't need meds or alcohol to pick me up and or help me come down. I don't crave anything that will change my personality. I went to hell and came out on fire. I arise in the morning and immediately get in the Bible so I can receive strength and direction for my day. I make a plan and walk out that plan. That's called consistency.

I cannot describe in words how excited I am every day to see the results of commitment and consistency. How could I ever doubt that I am in the center of His will for my life when I receive thousands of messages of deliverance, inner healing, and restored marriages?

You see a crazy, excited, impassioned woman on social media who screams about the goodness of God. What you don't see is the time I spend alone in His presence each day. I know this is what gives me the unction to do what I do.

I just told you that our God shows no partiality and plays no favorites. It's true. He simply rewards those who come to

Him and humbly ask, not for His hand, but for His glory. He qualifies whom He pleases and blesses those whom He loves.

It's never too late to give Him your *yes*. Think about it: the only thing you need to decide right now is not to turn back or bring your past into your future. Did you get that? *All you need is a made-up mind*. Nothing changes until something changes in you. You can cry, pray, pout, and get angry, but none of that works. What works is to help God help you.

Not all storms come to disrupt your life; some come to clear your path.

I think the enemy puts a defeated, hopeless spirit on us because He knows it's the only way he can stop us. He knows that once we get sick and tired of being sick and tired, we will finally do something about our situation and jump feet first into God's plan.

Knowing that makes me excited—excited about your new season and about your being the game changer God uses to break generational curses off your entire bloodline. No longer will you allow insecurity, intimidation, and frustration to rule your decisions. Only people who are insecure about their identity in Christ strive day and night to gain the approval of everyone around them. They do it because they want to feel better about themselves. They haven't yet discovered what you are learning: that not all storms come to disrupt your life; some come to clear your path. When you realize that you are already qualified by God to live your best life, you begin living for God first.

That opens a whole new world of opportunities. When you are secure in who God has called you to be, you will resist the outside demands and pressures that try to mold you into someone you can never become.

One of a Kind

Judges chapters 4 and 5 tell of a woman named Deborah who was a prophetess, a mighty warrior, and the only female judge. She was one of the most influential women of her day and the only woman in the Old Testament known for her faith and action apart from any relationship to her husband or any other man.

Deborah used to sit under the palm tree between Ramah and Bethel in Ephraim while the Israelites lined up to hear her wisdom on important matters. (See Judges 4:5.) She impresses me because she was unlike anyone in her day. She lived in a culture that believed women were subordinate to men, yet she spent her life seeking not God's hand but His face. Through her persistence, she became a leader in battle and a prophetess of the Lord who never demanded respect but earned the right to stand among men as an equal and a leader. Though she did not demand it, she received respect and honor throughout the nation. She knew that, in her own might, she could never have accomplished what God accomplished through her obedience, courage, and faith.

Deborah obviously understood the importance of the battle she fought. But she could not possibly have seen all its implications for history. If she had understood the larger magnitude of the battle, it would have made the fight easier. As it is, I can barely imagine the loneliness she must have felt, not only as the first woman judge over Israel, but also as a powerful woman—a warrior in a world where women were less likely to be out front. Nevertheless, she led Israel's army by faith, expecting God to come through. And He did. No man qualified Deborah. God qualified her.

You are no different from Deborah. God is qualifying you for your next battle. Winning will be your decision. When you realize that you are qualified, you will not allow the devil to abort your mission. You will not second-guess your decisions.

Yet, if I were to ask every reader, "Are you exactly where you thought you would be at this time in your life?" I'm sure most would answer with a resounding, "No."

I believe Deborah would have given the same answer. She could not have known that millennia later, we would tell her story and hail her as God's faithful instrument in the earth. Isn't that true of you? You have no idea what your story is about to look like or what it will look like centuries from now, should Jesus tarry. But you can rest assured of this: when you understand that God created you for *this* time and place, your story will unfold as the best seller He envisions.

You see, God is bigger than your misunderstandings and your missed opportunities. He is the God of the second, third, and fourth chance. When you receive this revelation, you will never again miss your God opportunity. But if you fail to see that God is working for you, you will abort your destiny. You will prematurely end the God move that is working for your future *now*.

All of us have done it. We abort the process because it's uncomfortable, painful, or even unpopular. But I dare you to be different in this season of your life. I challenge you to make the decisions that once seemed too uncomfortable. It's time to give God an opportunity to shake off your lethargy, fear, and hopelessness, because you are one of a kind and this is your season.

Understand Destiny

> Before I formed you in the womb I knew you; before you were born I sanctified you; I ordained you a prophet to the nations.
>
> —JEREMIAH 1:5

Destiny is the predetermined and predestined will of God for your life. God told Jeremiah that He knew him before he was formed in his mother's womb. God knew everything about Jeremiah and everything about his call.

You are as important to God as Jeremiah. Yet it's easy to become focused on your current storm and lose sight of what God is trying to do in and through you. (It happened to Jeremiah!) I have discovered that every season is either a lesson or a blessing. Your enemy the devil knows that if he can divert your focus from your purpose, he can steal your dream. He will use anyone and anything available to disrupt the flow of what God is doing in your life for His purposes.

When you understand the true meaning of your destiny, you become secure in who God made you to be. God uses all things to work together for good. Even when you go through painful transitions, God is setting you up for a trajectory shift in your life.

During my second divorce, I had no idea that I could ever be used by God again. Religion had told me that I was going to hell on a Slip 'N Slide. How in the world could someone twice divorced and unable to keep her own life together help other people change their lives? This was just one of the thousands of questions that played in my mind daily—that is, until I finally understood that Satan is the father of lies and cannot tell the truth. Therefore, I knew he could not offer me wisdom or advice about my divorce or ministry. He could not torment me with that scheme any longer.

I'm a living and breathing witness that God will pick you up right where you have fallen, dust you off, dress you up (like Cinderella), and present you to the prince of the ball.

You can be your own greatest supporter or your biggest critic. All human beings have a sinful nature. If you allow your natural self to disrupt your emotions and determine your path, you will never choose the higher road, which is the inner voice of the Holy Spirit. Therefore, when I get distracted and realize that I am being led by my emotions, I immediately lay hands on myself and tell that ugly spirit to line up with the God call in my life. I refuse to be led by emotions that wreak havoc in my life when I can live in peace and harmony within myself.

God has you on an incredible journey. Don't let distractions such as insecurity and self-doubt waylay your destiny. I try to be as transparent as possible because I want you to see living proof that God is good, even when we are our worst selves. I have a great life today, but I still have down days when I must discern what is happening and tell the devil to go back to hell, from whence he came. I still have to shut hell up when those inner voices try to take over my mind and rob me of my peace.

Even today, when I walk into a crowded building and hear people screaming my name, it's hard for me to believe that I am the event's special speaker. I stand in awe that God would use someone as fragile and broken as I was to deliver a word that sets people free. I can question the whys for the rest of my life; however, I have come to the realization that I could never be good enough to do what I do. It's just the grace of God that He chose me and allows me to be an instrument that He can use.

Your Part, His Promise

Understand that God has given you the opportunity to be unlike anyone else in your world. You were created to love, honor, and share Him with the people you meet. It doesn't matter what kind of degree you have or whether you have any degree at all. God chooses whom He pleases. People don't qualify you; God does.

Your part is to get in God's Word and begin to know Him. The facts in your life tell you one thing, but faith tells another! The doctor's report suggests one story, but the Word of God reveals another. Your bank account describes your current reality, but the Holy Spirit unveils your future. The promises in the Word are for you if you will believe!

Don't sweat the fight you've already won.

It's important to understand that people will never cease to disappoint you, even those who are closest to you. My husband and I have seen the people we thought were the closest to us leave us. We reeled in shock. In fact, those whom I expected to stick around forever were some of the first to jump ship. Sometimes, those who have been with you throughout your life will draw surprising conclusions without any explanation. The only sure promise you have in this life is that Jesus Christ will never leave nor forsake you.

I look back and think about how people wrote me off and were sleeping on (overlooking or disregarding) me and my comeback—the same way people are sleeping on you. Get the attitude I did: I stopped being mad at them for writing me off. I simply whispered to myself, "Get your rest."

> *Testimony*
>
> Work in progress! Fifty-seven years of me being a mess, talking about others, judging to make [myself] feel better while spending money to help satisfy the pains of my childhood. Being so mad at God for things that were not His fault. God didn't abuse me or make my dad drink. He isn't why my brother is a drug addict. Or why my mom is a narcissist. But I thought if God was real, He wouldn't allow these things to happen. RTK Inner Circle has made me look inside and see that I have a choice each day to be there. Miserable and angry–I don't live there anymore! I went to church for the first time in forty-three years last Sunday! Praise God! That's what Pastor Kim has done for me!
>
> –K

I can tell you that God will reward you in public for what you fought privately. Don't sweat the fight you've already won. I stopped focusing on people's support and focused on my growth and walk with God. I allowed myself to get free from needing people's support. I got so busy with being used by God and preparing for the things I'd prayed for that, when God saw I was ready, what He did blew my mind.

That is exactly what He is doing in and through you. The reason God trusted you with all the detours and storms that you've weathered will become clear when the time is right. Meanwhile, everything that happened has qualified you for something greater. It has qualified you to represent God, but with skin on.

I could not complete this journey with you without saying

that, no matter what, you can make it. He is saying to you today, "I trust you."

Now go and be. Be with no limits. Be all that God has created you to be. Put that seat belt on and fly, baby, fly.

Testimony

I've been listening to Real Talk Kim in the mornings while getting ready for work. Pastor Kim has given me the blessing of hope to look forward and not backward in my life. She has renewed a hope and expectancy in me and my life. She's real and she's been in the places we've been. I love her and I'm thankful that God led me to her. She preaches and the Word sticks with me. Through her, I have drawn closer to God and my trust in Him is being renewed. I just want to say, "Thank you" to God for blessing me with Pastor Kim.

–K

Today's Declaration

Lord, I decree and declare that my tomorrow will look nothing like my yesterday. I am being given the opportunity to be me, and I will be the best me ever created. I now give You all rule and reign over my life, home, family, and future. I am predestined to walk out Your plan, and I will do it to the best of my ability. The cross of Christ and the indwelling of His Spirit have set me free from all bondages. Even in my imperfection, I am complete in Christ my Lord, who rules and reigns forever and is the head of all principality and power.

Notes

Introduction

1. Steven Furtick, *(Un)Qualified: How God Uses Broken People to Do Big Things* (Colorado Springs: Multnomah Books, 2016), 8, https://www.google.com/books/edition/Un_qualified/hP3aCwAAQBAJ.
2. Furtick, *(Un)Qualified,* 9.
3. Furtick, *(Un)Qualified,* 9.
4. Furtick, *(Un)Qualified,* 149.

Chapter 1

1. John Hagee, *What Every Man Wants in a Woman: 10 Essentials for Growing Deeper in Love* (Lake Mary, FL: Charisma House, 2007), 3, https://books.google.com/books?id=NrSKU-XUBXsC.
2. Kimberly Jones-Pothier, *Beautifully Broken* (Bloomington, IN: AuthorHouse, 2015), chap. 1, https://www.google.com/books/edition/Beautifully_Broken/AEGlCAAAQBAJ.
3. Jones-Pothier, *Beautifully Broken,* chap. 1.
4. Furtick, *(Un)Qualified,* 8–9.

Chapter 2

1. Mary Jane Chaignot, "A Question about the Napkin Placed on Jesus' Face," BibleWise, accessed December 3, 2019, https://www.biblewise.com/bible_study/questions/a-question-about.php.

Chapter 3

1. Lights Poxlietner, "Quotable Quote," Goodreads, accessed December 11, 2019, https://www.goodreads.com/quotes/626779-honestly-if-you-don-t-fit-in-then-you-re-probably-doing.
2. Greg Herrick, "Introduction, Background, and Outline to Philippians," Bible.org, June 29, 2004, https://bible.org/seriespage/introduction-background-and-outline-philippians.
3. Rick Ezell, "Sermon: Rise Above Discouragement—Jeremiah 20," LifeWay, January 1, 2014, https://www.lifeway.com/en/articles/sermon-rise-above-discouragement-jeremiah-20. The text of this sermon inspired portions of this section.
4. Ezell, "Sermon: Rise Above Discouragement—Jeremiah 20."
5. Ezell, "Sermon: Rise Above Discouragement—Jeremiah 20."
6. Ezell, "Sermon: Rise Above Discouragement—Jeremiah 20."
7. Ezell, "Sermon: Rise Above Discouragement—Jeremiah 20."
8. Ezell, "Sermon: Rise Above Discouragement—Jeremiah 20."

Chapter 4

1. Trent Shelton, "Refuse to Be Used," YouTube, December 6, 2018, 3:04, https://www.youtube.com/watch?v=Ry-uUEZBTkU.

Chapter 6

1. John Ortberg, *Everybody's Normal Till You Get to Know Them* (Grand Rapids, MI: Zondervan, 2003), chap. 4,

https://www.google.com/books/edition/Everybody_s_Normal_Till_You_Get_to_Know/ZF0SXdk_h4sC.

Chapter 7

1. "Review & Giveaway: *Alec* by L. A. Casey (Blog Tour)," Bad Bird Reads, October 30, 2014, https://badbirdreads.com/review-giveaway-alec-l-casey-blog-tour/.
2. SuMMit CrossFit, Facebook, July 30, 2019, https://m.facebook.com/SuMMitCrossFit/posts/2320702031318339.

Chapter 8

1. Chana Weisberg, "Nitzevet, Mother of David: The Bold Voice of Silence," Chabad.org, accessed December 8, 2019, https://www.chabad.org/theJewishWoman/article_cdo/aid/280331/jewish/Nitzevet-Mother-of-David.htm.
2. Weisberg, "Nitzevet, Mother of David."
3. Weisberg, "Nitzevet, Mother of David."
4. Weisberg, "Nitzevet, Mother of David."
5. Weisberg, "Nitzevet, Mother of David."
6. "This may have some reference to David's preferment; he was the stone which Saul and his courtiers rejected, but was by the wonderful providence of God advanced to be the headstone of the building. But its principal reference is to Christ." Matthew Henry, "Commentary on Psalms 118," Blue Letter Bible, accessed December 8, 2019, https://www.blueletterbible.org/Comm/mhc/Psa/Psa_118.cfm?a=596022.
7. Weisberg, "Nitzevet, Mother of David."
8. Rick Warren, *God's Power to Change Your Life* (Grand Rapids, MI: Zondervan, 2006), 12, https://www.google.com/books/edition/God_s_Power_to_Change_Your_Life/AzqX0UvwOvMC.
9. Warren, *God's Power to Change Your Life*, 12.

10. Warren, *God's Power to Change Your Life,* 13.
11. Warren, *God's Power to Change Your Life,* 14–15.
12. Warren, *God's Power to Change Your Life,* 15–16.
13. Warren, *God's Power to Change Your Life,* 16.

Chapter 9

1. Joel Osteen, "No More Excuses—Joel Osteen," *Anointed Messages Sermon Notes,* February 14, 2015, http://anointedmessagesnotes.blogspot.com/2015/02/no-more-excuses-joel-osteen.html.
2. Osteen, "No More Excuses—Joel Osteen."
3. "Facts and Figures," Alzheimer's Association, accessed December 12, 2019, https://www.alz.org/alzheimers-dementia/facts-figures.
4. Erica Roth, "7 Tips for Reducing Sundowning," Healthline, August 16, 2016, https://www.healthline.com/health/dementia-sundowning.

Chapter 10

1. "What Is a Hurt, Habit, or Hang-Up?" Celebrate Recovery, New Hope Church, accessed December 10, 2019, https://www.cr.newhope.org/what-is-a-hurt-habit-or-hang-up.
2. "Show Me Your Hand," Theological Stew, accessed December 12, 2019, http://www.theologicalstew.com/show-me-your-hand.html.
3. "Show Me Your Hand," Theological Stew.

Chapter 11

1. Apple of God's Eye (@itzTheAppleeye), Twitter, July 9, 2018, 12:50 a.m., https://twitter.com/itzTheAppleeye/status/1016228119227830272.

2. Trent Shelton (@TrentShelton), Twitter, May 25, 2019, 5:48 p.m., https://twitter.com/TrentShelton/status/1132448424870252555.
3. Osteen, "No More Excuses—Joel Osteen."
4. Osteen, "No More Excuses—Joel Osteen."
5. Osteen, "No More Excuses—Joel Osteen."
6. "These 4 Studies Show How Porn-Obsessed Brains Can Heal Over Time," Fight the New Drug, April 22, 2019, https://fightthenewdrug.org/4-studies-that-prove-porn-addicted-brains-can-return-to-normal/,

Chapter 12

1. Joyce Meyer, "Learning to Fly," *Christian Today*, November 9, 2007, https://www.christiantoday.com/article/joyce.meyer.learning.to.fly/14484.htm. Meyer's article inspired this discussion.

Chapter 13

1. Benjamin Hollis, "Armor," *Victori*: The Roman Military, accessed December 12, 2019, https://romanmilitary.net/tools/armor/.

Chapter 14

1. Emil G. Hirsch et al., "Solomon," *Jewish Encyclopedia*, accessed December 11, 2019, http://www.jewishencyclopedia.com/articles/13842-solomon.

MY FREE GIFT TO YOU

When the Enemy Brings Up Your Past, Remind Him of Your Future

I am so happy you read my book. I hope this book helped you to use what God says about you to fight negative self-talk and lies from the enemy.

As my way of saying *thank you*...
I am offering you a gift:

E-book: *Conquering the Obstacles*

To get this FREE GIFT, please go to
WWW.SHUTHELLUP.COM/GIFT

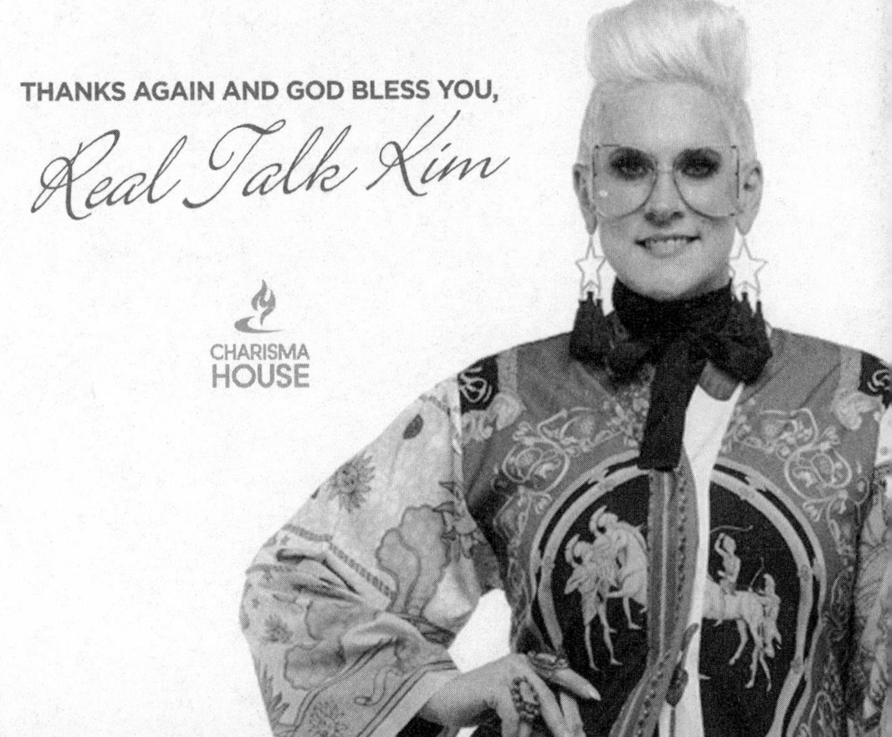

THANKS AGAIN AND GOD BLESS YOU,

Real Talk Kim

CHARISMA HOUSE